LIFE'S GREAT
ADVENTURE

LIFE'S GREAT ADVENTURE

A guide to living an adventurous, purposeful life, whatever your passion.

Deri Llewellyn-Davies

MAKE YOUR MARK GLOBAL

MAKE YOUR MARK GLOBAL PUBLISHING, LTD

USA & Monaco

Life's Great Adventure 2nd edition © 2017-19 Deri Llewellyn-Davies

Library of Congress Cataloging-in-Publication Data

Library of Congress Control Number: 2017913086

Life's Great Adventure: A guide to living an adventurous, purposeful life, whatever your passion.

First edition: December 2012

Fernley, Nevada

Publisher: Make Your Mark Global, LTD

p. 268

Trade Paperback ISBN 0-9980745-5-1

Subjects: Self-help techniques

Summary: This book is born from a passion and a crash course in life lessons whilst experiencing some of this earth's greatest challenges. Extreme adventure can reveal who we truly are. (For most, thankfully, it is not the only way.) When you throw yourself amongst the elements, stripping yourself bare of all needless material wants, pitting yourself in a battle of survival where the next breath, the next step, is all that matters breaking yourself physically, mentally and emotionally the only thing that is left is you and your spirit. From this place, the soul can reveal itself. Your truth, your essence, is fully revealed in all its glory, provided you are ready and able to listen.

Printed in the USA & United Kingdom

Table of Contents

Dedication

This is written for my beautiful daughters, Aarrowen Devine, Eliona Seren and Maddisynne Mai. Live your passions every day. You have taught me love beyond words; you are all my number one passion.

Preface

This book is born from a passion and a crash course in life lessons whilst experiencing some of this earth's greatest challenges. It started out as a journal to capture the essence of what I have achieved and what I have experienced and learnt along the way. It then became a project born out of my wanting to share my key lessons in life and my great adventures with my children and grandchildren—to leave a legacy of the mind that will encourage, motivate and inspire them to their own unique greatness. To show them they can really do anything they set their minds to. I want them to dream big and aim for the stars.

As this book progressed, it became evident that although it was to be a book about my varied adventures in my 'big adventure'—life—it was going to be far more than that. Its essence clearly became that of life lessons and the potential for personal evolution. This became most evident in the last few chapters where you will be presented with quite a twist and revelation in my own life and way of thinking. It has been an exhilarating experience writing this as it has refocused me on old lessons, taught me all the lessons afresh, and realigned me personally and professionally.

This book slowly evolved into something that I knew would be of huge benefit to others, not just to my kids and grandchildren. And seeing as my grandchildren are a long way off and my daughters cannot read yet, the lessons seemed wasted at this stage. So, Life's Great Adventure has now been purposefully designed to help you too—it is my gift to the world. I will take you inside my personal adventures and let you experience the lessons along the way through a gripping tale of action adventure and a true discovery of mind, body and spirit.

Some of the world's great leaders and teachers have at some point gone through a period of silence, of wilderness or of self-destruction even—a breaking of the human essence, mentally, physically or emotionally, or in my case all three. Now I do not claim to be a world's great by any stretch of the imagination. I can, however, relate to how this process can reveal one's inner soul. We are all so busy in our lives, so distracted by everything around us in the Western world. Information is coming to us at light speed as we find ourselves immersed in technology. Somewhere along the way we have lost connection with our souls, our spirit, and with our godlike connection to who we really are and why we are living.

Extreme adventure can reveal who we truly are. (For most, thankfully, it is not the only way.) When you throw yourself amongst the elements, stripping yourself bare of all needless material wants, pitting yourself in a battle of survival where the next breath, the next step, is all that matters—breaking yourself physically, mentally and emotionally— the only thing that is left is you and your spirit. From this place, the soul can reveal itself. Your truth, your essence, is fully revealed in all its glory, provided you are ready and able to listen. Such was my experience on many an adventurous occasion.

My journey has been a profound one, through the Sahara Desert and to the tops of some of the highest mountains in the world. The journey continues and no doubt will never cease. When I started this journey, it was born out of ego, out of a desire for challenge, drive and great goals. It was a journey I was meant to conquer, with challenges I was meant to smash. The reality would become evident very quickly as I was brought to my knees, reduced to tears and humbled on many occasions along the way, and this, I am sure, will also continue. I never set out on this quest to learn life's great lessons, and at the time I did not take them in fully. But, on reflection, I am amazed at how much I have absorbed these lessons into my life and what they have done for me.

My soul's calling was through adventure—extreme adventure— but everyone is unique. Your calling or 'thing' may be yoga, your work, your spouse, sport, career, giving, serving, religion, spirit, creation— golf. Whatever your calling is, go there and invest wholeheartedly, 100%. It is there you will find yourself. This book will guide you through that journey of self- discovery and take you on your own great adventure. You deserve it! And right now is your time.

I am sure you will enjoy reading this book as much as I have enjoyed writing it. Please remember, though, this is not an adventure book with life lessons—it is a book that shares lessons in life through adventure. I suggest you take the adventure as a metaphor as I have intended.

The lessons contained herein are applicable to all areas of life, and I certainly use them as such.

I hope this book will guide you on your own adventure to discover your true passion and purpose, and to finally take the action to become who you truly are and fully deserve to be. Ultimately, its purpose is to help you to realise your full potential in this lifetime. I wish you well on your journey, and I urge you to live it fully. We have but one chance at this life; our fleeting presence is gone so swiftly. Live fully whilst you are here, and when the final calling comes, know that you can go with a smile on your face, with no regrets. As my story will reveal, I would much rather live with failure than regret. (More on that later; I better not spoil things.)

On a final note, this book is now a gift in more ways than I had originally intended. In alignment with my core belief that all children deserve a safe, fair and empowered existence, I have decided to donate 100% of my author profits from the sale of *Life's Great Adventure* to *Global Angels* (www.globalangels.com). Global Angels has a BIG vision, and you know I like big visions! For me that's the icing on the cake for writing *Life's Great Adventure*.

May your God bless you on your journey. Enjoy the ride!

Yours in Adventure!

Deri ap John Llewellyn-Davies

Introduction

"I could see no one either ahead or behind; I was truly alone in the vast expanse of the Sahara. Having completed nearly four marathons in four days whilst carrying everything I needed to survive, and with over two marathons to go in the 'toughest footrace on earth', I had nothing left. I was broken, physically and emotionally. It was just me and my spirit, or what was left of it, remaining.

In the midst of the Sahara Desert, I dropped my pack and collapsed onto my knees on the sand, spent. I looked up to the heavens, to the overwhelming beauty of the stars and the universe, and just shouted, 'Why the BLEEP am I doing this? Why me? If I am truly meant to do this, then give me a sign because I'm done!' ... Then the unexpected happened. I got my answer..."

Before we begin our journey together, I encourage you to ask yourself these simple questions:

What is the purpose of life?

Why do I exist?

What do I really want to do in this lifetime before I die?

What do I want to see, do, feel and experience?

If I am lying on my deathbed with a smile on my face, what have I achieved that has made me so happy and fulfilled, ready to meet my maker?

If I am at my 100th birthday party, what do I want people to say about me? How do I want to be introduced?

Now do not panic. I am only teasing. I know these are not simple questions at all! They are the fundamental questions of life, some of the toughest questions any of us can face. But face them we will as we progress through this book. As you acknowledge your own answers to these questions, you will find yourself taking action, daily, to live your life by your answers. So, by the time you reach the last page, you will be immersed in life's great adventure— your adventure— living a life of purpose and fulfilment. This book will be your guide.

I did the same exercise, answering these questions, many years ago, and I repeat the process regularly as the answers change subtly with age and experience. One of the themes that kept raising its head for me was *global adventure*: the highest mountains on earth, the two Poles, the infamous desert and jungle races. This was one theme, and of course there were other areas of my life: *abundance, relationships, health, passion, travel, philanthropy* and *home* had similar grand illusions. This adventure theme, however, was the one that 'hurt' the most. It was a passion, a calling to me from deep within my very soul, and yet I was doing nothing towards it.

Why? Mostly because of fear, excuses, a busy lifestyle, cannot afford it, not fit enough … the list went on.

The question that had the biggest impact on me at that time was the deathbed question. If I was laying on my deathbed, looking back over my life, what would I be proud of? What would I remember and what would I regret? Would I remember all those countless hours in the office, the commuting time or nights in the pub? Or would I remember the precise moment and feeling as I crossed the finish line of the toughest footrace on earth or summited one of the highest mountains? The answer was clear.

"Live a life of no regret"

The Global Grand Slam

From that moment, I vowed I would steadily and consistently apply myself to achieving the greatest challenges on earth — what I call *'The Global Adventurer's Grand Slam'*. This is a growing list, but at present it consists of The Marathon des Sables (243 km, Sahara Desert, Morocco), The Jungle Marathon (200 km, Manaus, Amazonia and Brazil), Ironman Triathlon, The Seven Summits[1] and both poles. Why these? I don't know.

---

[1] The Seven Summits comprise the highest peaks on each of Earth's seven continents: Asia - Mt. Everest, 8850 metres; South America - Aconcagua, 6962 metres; North America – Denali (Mt. McKinley), 6194 metres; Africa - Kilimanjaro, 5895 metres; Europe - Mt. Elbrus, 5642 metres; Antarctica - Vinson Massif, 4897 metres; Australia - Mt. Kosciuszko, 2228 metres.

It's what calls me. It's what excites me, like why I love vegemite but hate marmite. I just do. And I have no idea why, and that's just part of the magic.

I have been steadily pursuing my dream, and this book is about the journey and magical life lessons I learnt along the way, mostly unintentionally. These are all fundamental life lessons that, when weaved together as a whole, provide the entire blueprint to live a fulfilled life of great adventure. And please remember, I use the term 'adventure' as a metaphor in the context of life.

The actual definition of **ad ven ture [ad-ven-cher] – noun** in the dictionary is:

1. An exciting, daring or very unusual experience.

2. Participation in exciting undertakings or enterprises: the spirit of adventure.

3. A bold, usually risky undertaking; hazardous action with uncertain outcome.

4. A commercial or financial speculation of any kind; venture.

5. A risk or a hazard.

6. To take the chance of, to dare.

Participating in exciting undertakings can relate to anything in life, so I encourage you to start to think about which adventure in life you wish to embark upon. It may be a relationship, new home, new job, new business, travel or indeed a mountain. Whatever your adventure, let's begin it.

Life's great lessons, chapter by chapter

I am a great student of personal growth and development. I bring three decades of study, tens of thousands of pounds worth of education, and progressive application and experience. I can see that my life lessons mirror those of some of the great masters in personal evolution. Yet, despite hearing a lot of these lessons in different ways and in different formats over the years, it finally took Mother Earth herself to teach me the lessons the hard way for me to truly take them on board and internalise them. And to date I have not seen all these lessons woven together in one place for total absorption; hence, another reason for developing this book.

I have learnt and lived these lessons to the very core of who I am, so I find the stories so compelling. My hope is that for you they will be unforgettable and will give you the inspiration and recall to apply the teachings. Each chapter contains a unique adventure, a key lesson and numerous 'aha's'. In addition, I have woven in the lessons of some of my greatest teachers to complement my own experience and to give you additional resources to expand your learning further. Each chapter concludes with a selection of exercises that can assist you to absorb and apply the lessons in your own life. More on that later.

Each chapter is a story in its own right, and the lessons embedded within each adventure build to an unforgettable crescendo. The sequence of lessons is important, like a magic formula—if applied in the wrong sequence, it can have a very different result. Just like starting a goal without a vision or purpose.

You could end up way off the mark and spinning your wheels. So, I strongly encourage you to read the book from front cover to back cover.

Do take notice and reflect on the order of things within the book, as it is purposeful. Like baking a cake, if you throw the flour in at the wrong time the whole cake can be far from appetising—yet all the ingredients were the same. Such is life. Have you noticed that some people appear to have all the right ingredients, possibly the same as someone else they compare themselves with, and yet one person has it all and the other doesn't?

What makes the difference? Is it education? I know people who went to the same school or university, with the same course and grades, but one is on welfare and one is highly successful. Is it upbringing? Well, there are many success stories of people from poor backgrounds achieving just as well as many rich kids, rich kids who go off the rails and end up junkies. Is it looks? Is it luck?

The only thing to me that makes any sense in what I have seen in life, and on the mountains, is our mind. And that is the one thing in life we are actually in control of—our thoughts—yet most of us do not know it. Therein lays the difference between those who succeed and those who do not.

Please stop just a moment and think about this. Whether you think you can succeed or think you cannot, you will be proven right! You will be what you think. So before we start the first chapter in earnest, I really implore you to think and to open your mind, just a little bit, to the possibilities of success. Even if only for the brief moments you have picked up this book, feel free now to put it down and reflect…

I know the lessons I share can truly change your life for the better. They have worked for me and those close to me, my clients and my friends, and it can for you. It all begins with a thought, a little thought, a positive thought. A thought that maybe there is something more. *Maybe I deserve happiness and fulfilment, maybe … just maybe…* a little hope. Let's build from there.

Hold this thought as we progress through the chapters, and all will become clear by the final chapter when we revisit this concept in a much more holistic way.

But for now, just **start paying attention to your thoughts**, each and every day. You really are what you think. You are the sum total of your thoughts, past, present and future. If you think bad things always happen to you, they usually will. You know the kind of person you avoid who is always down and negative?

Well, guess what? They are always down and negative!

Now, that could be you! I believe we are our vibration, and we attract to ourselves those who vibrate at a similar level. So take a good look around you. Who are you attracting? Are you attracting magic into your life and wonderful people who help you grow and inspire you to new and great things? Or are you attracting losers who just make you feel worse than you already do and suck the life energy out of you? That's just something to think about.

I do not want to delve into this too much here as the concept will evolve and expand in the following chapters. But I want to just pop these thoughts into your mind for now. This topic of the Law of Attraction has become quite mainstream of late with a book/ DVD called *The Secret*. If you have read or watched this, then that's great. If not, I highly encourage you to get a copy. It will set up a great context for this book, particularly the concept that our thoughts create our reality. However, know there are other laws too… like the law of ACTION ;-)

YOU can be an action-taker in your own adventure

TRUE Thinking – Discover the TRUE you

Have you ever found that when you become inspired by the adventures in other people's lives, you often wish that you could follow in their footsteps? That's the same for most people, but 97% of today's society never reaches their full potential. Why? Because they do not know how to choose the right thoughts, make important decisions, and take action on their desires.

Through my unique combination of expertise and experience in both the business and extreme sports industries, I have been able to hone in on the essential keys for success—and they all start with our *thinking*.

So, as promised, this is not just a story of my adventure, and it also is not a book where lessons and stories are given with no clear application. It is a book to help you take off on your own personal adventure in life through a whole new way of exploring, based on TRUE Thinking and drawing on my adventure as inspiration.

How to use this book

At the end of each chapter, we facilitate your own personal exploration and growth through exercises that will stretch you, test you and guide you on your own great adventure. These will be broken down into four sections to ensure we capture the whole essence of you. We will explore and probe from all angles: body, mind and subconscious. (Yes, I know 'probe' sounds a bit invasive, but change does not come without some discomfort. I can assure you, the rewards at the end are worth it!)

So, not only will you be coming on an adventure with me, but you will be creating your own along the way. Now, it is up to you how you engage with the book. You could diligently work through all the exercises after each chapter, or come back after you have read the whole book and work through them then. I personally believe that the end of each chapter is the perfect time to attempt the exercises as each chapter will inspire you and put you in a state of belief in your own abilities. Whichever approach you choose, however, I urge you to commit to doing the exercises. I promise you, it will make a difference.

Now, there are four basic things I discovered (often the hard way) that you absolutely need to do to prepare for, and succeed in, an action-based exploration or adventure:

✓ Do not forget the torch and the batteries! You need to see where you are going.

✓ You need to map out your journey if you want to reach your destination.

✓ It is a good idea to consult others who have gone before you (read guide books, 'Google' your destination, learn of the pitfalls along the way)

✓ Do not forget your compass or GPS (a working one!) — and your common sense.

Along this vein, let's have a quick look at the four key action tasks/exercises in each chapter that will facilitate complete personal exploration from four different angles:

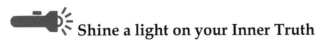 Shine a light on your Inner Truth

Here, we will explore your real inner truth. No bull. No make-believe, No Hollywood myth, just your core beliefs. The real, true you. Be prepared to strap in and face some challenging and awe-inspiring questions and processes.

Map out your True Path

Once you know who you truly are, you will need to map out your True Path to follow. Your path encompasses your passions, visions and goals—your direction in life and focus. In this section you will gain clarity and begin that journey on your very own True Path.

Refer to your True Guide to lead the way

Once you are getting clear on your Inner Truth and are on your True Path, you will next need True Guides along the way. These can come in many forms: outer guides such as friends, coaches and mentors, and inner guides such as your conscience or inner knowing.

It is time to reflect, to get good advice and to have accountability to a higher power.

Identify your inner True North

The final icing on the cake is a deeper inner connection, mostly known as your 'gut feeling' or, as I call it, your 'True North'. We will explore instinct, intuition and coincidence and really connect you to your True North.

You will find that in life you predominantly use one of these methods when making decisions. Therefore, you may find you are drawn to do just one or a select few of these exercises at the end of each chapter. That's cool. There's no right or wrong. However, I will tell you, results are completely transformed when you start using TRUE Thinking which encompasses all four approaches. You see, when you get to think about yourself from so many different angles, using all your senses and all of your brain, you will explore fully and have a much more holistic approach and outcome.

I invite you to journey with me through *Life's Great Adventure*. We are going to begin with rediscovering your passion and your purpose in life through some early childhood adventures. We'll then move on to build confidence and belief through some small beginnings in marathons and the National Three Peaks Challenge. A grand vision will be charted as we progress through the Inca Trail and the start of the Seven Summits. Your own specific goals will be defined and clarified as we endure the legendary Marathon des Sables, one step at a time. Preparation and patience will be rediscovered on the great white peak of Kilimanjaro.

Then it starts getting tough. We will need to deal with the crippling fear that stops us in the Alps and how to make and live with tough decisions in Russia on Mount Elbrus. We then travel deep into the heart of Alaska, dealing with a failure in life on Denali. Finally, it all comes together in the Andes, on the slopes of Aconcagua discovering how to 'feel it now', to enjoy the journey.

So, take a deep breath and get ready to discover the TRUE you. Let the adventure begin.

PS: As this book inspires you to craft your own epic life of adventure, visit www.DiamondLifeDesign.com to download your free life design template. It's the exact framework I use personally to create a life of no regrets!

Chapter 1

A Childhood Adventure

DREAMING BIG AND DISCOVERING YOUR PASSION

Happy are those who dream dreams and are ready to pay the price to make them come true.
~ Leon J. Suenes

"It was a whiteout. The storm was raging all around. Already several members of the team had frostbite as we battled our way back to camp from a failed summit bid. We were balancing precariously at 20,000 ft in deepest Alaska, with temperatures below -40. This was the legendary Denali Pass, one of the coldest and most inhospitable places on earth. As legend goes, people have literally been flash-frozen here, and now I know why. I was on the very edge, literally, as we tried to make our way back along a tiny glacier edge. At the top of the raging storm, I was totally snow-blinded and my goggles had frozen. Each step was a gamble.

As I took one more step, there was suddenly nothing below me. A split second of weightlessness, of peace, and then I plummeted into an abyss. Below were thousands of feet of pure glacier and certain death. Realisation kicked in fast, adrenalin faster still, as I thrashed wildly to do an ice axe self-arrest, wishing dearly that I had paid more attention in the lessons and practiced more on the baby slopes. I slid now, picking up speed down the side of the glacier, shouting to my comrades who I was roped to, praying one would hear in the din of the storm raging all around…

As in any great adventure, this journey begins with one small step, a baby step, and you never know quite where that next step will take you; that is part of the magic."

Adversity is a blessing

Right from the moment I was born, I faced adversity. I was taken from my birth mother and put up for adoption. As a newborn I must have faced some emotional turmoil over this. But it would not be until years later that I truly understood the full implications. In hindsight, the whole experience was the best thing that could have happened to me. Wonderful parents adopted me. My mother and father were the best anyone could have wished for; I was brought up with love, care, values and morals. If my birth mother had brought me up, my life would have been very different; definitely not for the better. She was young and could not have supported me properly. I dread to think where I would be now. I have since met and built a wonderful relationship with her, and she is a wonderful person. But the tough decision she made (or was made for her) many years ago was the best decision, even though it must have torn her apart.

I open myself and my heart to you right from the beginning for a reason. From the very start of our journey together, I want to be totally open and transparent with you. In order for me to serve you fully, I need to bare my soul. This is a book about discovering your purpose in life, really living it, and being true to yourself. To get that message across, I need to be totally transparent in my own journey and share the adversities I went through, and overcame, as I sought to fulfil my passion. Do not be surprised, then, if you see this word, 'adversity', again!

Truly living your passion is a commitment not many people are willing to take, and it won't be a fairground ride. By committing to your deepest purpose and passions, you will face opposition. You will face obstacles and fear, and you will have to make some tough decisions. Like my adoption, sometimes it will be years later when you realise the full implication of earlier decisions made and that ultimately they were for the greater good.

No matter where you are in your life and what you face right now, you can change it with a decision now. A decision that you deserve more, that there is more to life, whatever that means to you. Then be prepared to take baby steps towards your dream, starting right now. Some of those steps may not be easy; some decisions will be tough, and you may even face fear head-on. I am here as your own Adventure Guide to help you through that journey, your own adventure in life, and to help prepare you for the pitfalls.

As a result of my adoption, I faced turmoil through my childhood, being called a 'bastard' by my supposed school friends in Hook CP, and even by my grandmother. I grew up with an uncertainty about who I was. But it is those tough times that have ultimately driven and served me. This uncertainty in my identity was a true gift. It drove me forward on a journey of self-discovery and a quest for self-knowledge, and it led me to ultimately write this book. So, to all those who cussed me in those early days, I thank you.

It is not what you face in life that determines who you are. It is how you 're-act' to it. In your 're-acting' you are in fact 're-en-acting' what has gone before, and it is your choice whether you choose for that to serve you or sink you. For many years my adoption was my Achilles heel, a sore point that just wasn't discussed. It wasn't until my early twenties, when I had finally found my birth mother and subsequently birth father, that I could look back with perspective and see my whole life thus far for what it was — a miracle.

So, instead of bitching and moaning about being adopted and resenting it in some way, I suddenly felt truly blessed and fully grateful. I could see the synchronicity at play, the pure chance of my birth mother being in Pembrokeshire to have the baby and the subtle magic at play for my parents to ultimately have me. How lucky I am, and I feel blessed every single day as a result. Despite your circumstances, try to get some perspective and some gratitude for where you are in your life, no matter how hard that may feel right now. It is in these small seeds of gratitude where the adventure truly begins.

Dream big

I wanted to open the book with a clear message: *Whatever it is you are facing right now, wherever you are, there is hope.*

There is a new life to be discovered, a new way, a new thought, a new feeling. I am here to guide you through the course of this book, and I will open myself fully, revealing the turmoil I have faced along the way. This is so you know that, sure, it is not going to be all sunshine and roses, but the next time you face a rainstorm you can do so with a smile on your face as you let it wash you and cleanse you.

Life's Great Adventure has been written to inspire you on your own adventure, whatever that may be. I want you to put down your baggage for a moment and start to think what is possible. No doubts, no fears, no excuses. We will deal with them in later chapters, but just for a moment, let's make the impossible possible.

From the very start, I will encourage you to start thinking about your own dreams, goals and aspirations. This will help you decide which adventures you are going to take off on! Some may already be clear in your mind, others a distant haze in your once passionate memory. Your dreams could be to visit some place in the world, like the pyramids, to climb a mountain (then you will definitely love my stories), to own a certain car, to find the perfect partner, to set up a business, to change job, to have the dream home, to build your confidence, or all of these! There are exercises at the end of this chapter that will help guide you through the process of choosing your goals. We will then begin to build the bigger picture of your loves and passions in the chapters and corresponding exercises that follow.

I am constantly adding to my vision and goals; this whole process is an evolution. Just last week, I saw a picture of Angkor Wat in Cambodia in a magazine, so that went straight on the 'Things To Do Before I Die' list. Now is the time for you to start making your own ever-expanding dream list, and have fun with it. This book is all about making these dreams come alive, bringing them into reality, baby step by baby step.

Discovering your passions

Perhaps you are like me and some of your goals or dreams are to climb a mountain or run 10 k or a marathon. These are goals and part of your life's great adventure but are not the adventure itself. Perhaps you need to go back to the beginning to discover your own true adventure, or to put it another way, your true passion.

Defining your overarching passion is important, although in some instances the passion can be quite narrow and defined. For me, my passion is extreme, action-based adventure, and that comes in many forms, from climbing mountains to crossing deserts, from local trekking to exploring the wonders of the world.

My passion is very broad; hence, I can be fulfilling it constantly as there will always be something to explore and define. A passion really is something that doesn't end, unlike a goal like climbing Elbrus where you do it once and it is done. A passion is never satiated; it lives with us and burns within us until we die.

Some passions can be narrow, like passion for piano. But, again, there is always a striving to be better, to learn more and do more, which never ceases. Passions do change, particularly with age. My daughters are now my top passion whereas it used to be rugby, which I no longer play or indeed watch much these days. (Unless Wales are playing!)

We need to look back at a time when we experienced true joy and freedom, true passion. For most, this would involve going all the way back to childhood. It is in fact in childhood that we first developed a true taste for adventure. What was it that you loved back then and still love and secretly covet? Perhaps it is time to rediscover that childhood dream and adventure and start to live it now.

But before we do skip back to the days of our childhood dreams and adventures, there is just one more point to share. Previously I referred to the 'ever- expanding' list of goals. To some people, like me ten years ago, to hear that could be a tough pill to swallow! *What? You don't one day get it all done? ...* No! You never get it done; life is about continuously creating and expanding. Like any life form (think plant), the day you stop growing and expanding is the day you die, and this is a book about living, truly living today. So, we have a continuously evolving list of things we are doing and will do with this wonderful gift of life.

No feeling stressed or anxious about the list and what has not been done, but revelling in the now, savouring the moment and being excited about what's next, constantly. ... But you will have to wait until the final chapter to see how that fully plays out in my own life.

If you are a slave to the to-do list, then I urge you to let it go. The list will never be done, and that is just fine.

You just focus on the now, do the things on the list which are appropriate and most important for today, make sure some of them are bringing you closer to your dreams (more on that later), and then sleep easy knowing you have had a great day.

Back to the beginning

I have had some revelations in the past few years, which we will come to all in good time as I do not wish to spoil the end of this tale. But, needless to say, I think for a lot of us our true sense of adventure began to surface as children. The big question is, when or where did we lose it? Think back to when you were a child, or even take a look around you at your own children or those around you — they are true, little adventurers in every way.

When my eldest daughter, Aarrowen was two, she is the apple of her daddy's eye and a truly magnificent adventurer. From the moment she woke, she wanted to explore the house, go outside, find new things and do new things; she was totally fearless. I have had numerous occasions where she has been standing on top of the stairs or a table, or whatever height she has managed to climb to, and she will just say "Daddy!" to get my attention and then fearlessly throw herself off into my arms with no thought as to whether or not I can actually get there to catch her in time. Thankfully, I have not missed one yet! If we go somewhere new, the playground, zoo or county fair, she wants to explore everything, from the piece of grass at her feet to the fairground carousel.

What a magnificent lesson we can learn from children: Be excited about each and every day, each and every moment. Just last month whilst at a local show, Aarrowen just stopped, pointed and said, "What's that?"(Her favourite phrase at present) as she honed in on the fairground swing. She then proceeded to drag me halfway across the fair with very clear intentions as to where she was going. She wanted that ride. We had not been to a fair before and this was the first fairground ride she'd seen. So she pestered me for several minutes to let her have a go. Now at this point in her life, she could not yet speak properly, so this involved 'Daddy' and 'want' with lots of vigorous pointing and a few tears. I tried to explain to her that it was for bigger children and was a little fast and she probably would not like it. But I really do not know why I was even attempting logical argument with a very small child. In the end, I decided she needed to follow her own path, and I just needed to support her.

I had a word with the owner, as Aarrowen was a little young, greased his palm and settled Aarrowen onto the ride. So there she was, happy as Larry. The ride started and around she went, all smiles, sparkles and magic! After the first circular revolution, the big smile had turned into a frown. On the second lap, the frown had turned into a grimace with the start of tears. Then, on the third revolution, it was full-on tears with some struggle to get out. Needless to say, Daddy was at hand, the ride was stopped, and that was the fastest £2.50 I have ever spent. A quick cuddle from Daddy and all was okay as she then pottered off to the next adventure without a care in the world—another fairground ride, bigger and faster! True brilliance, true adventure.

What do we have here in a child? A total fascination with life, with each moment a new discovery, total fearlessness, constant willingness to try something new and the ability to deal swiftly with failure and move onto the next thing. If we were all like that once, where did all that insatiable curiosity and drive go? And more importantly, how do we get it back? By the end of this book, it is my hope that you will be a fearless little adventurer again, if you are not already. And if you are, great! The adventures will just get bigger and better.

Now think about Aarrowen and the fairground ride. Sometimes the thing we think we want so badly and go all out for actually is not what it was cracked up to be. Or perhaps we even fail (heaven forbid!) at getting what we want. So, what next? Oftentimes we wallow in self-pity, cry at the failure or vow never to try anything ever again as this time it did not work out. Oh, what a sad life that is. Well, now it is time to flick the switch.

As we each look back at our life and our childhood, let's dust off all those old failures, and when something doesn't work out, let's just get back up and try it again, or try something different just as we did as children.

Sometimes we just have to try something to know we do not really want to do it. (This also applies to boyfriends and girlfriends)

That is why later in the book I spend several chapters on decision making, dealing with fear and coping with failure.

And as I dangle from a rope high in the Alps, scared shitless, I discover I really do not like rock climbing after all.

For now, though, let's just start trying to think like a child again. On writing this, last week Aarrowen did it again, similar ride, different fair, same insistency and same result—tears. But I can guarantee, at some point soon she will get back on the ride and love it! Such is life.

What does adventure mean to you?

The word *adventure* conjures many images, and I suppose it means many different things to each person. As I said before, your adventure is your passion. For me, it is *touching the greatest, most inaccessible places on this earth and following in the footsteps of legends.* So within this adventure or passion, there are a great many little adventures to go on.

In my childhood, like most young boys, I began reading books and watching films of great action adventures, often playing the hero. Funnily, though, I was to later learn in life that when you are actually on such an adventure, being a hero is the farthest thing from your mind. But back then, adventure to me was action and being a hero.

Adventure to me now also encompasses my relationships, my fiscal abundance, following my passions in business, and my health and vitality. In this book, however, we will focus on my real-life extreme sporting and action adventures and passions, following the more classical definition of an adventure. I use my own 'real' storybook adventures as a metaphor to bring the lessons contained therein to the front of your mind.

What does adventure mean to you? What are you passionate about? Really think about it. Your life's adventure can be anything you want it to be. It could be your career, an adventure in love, travelling to see the wonders of the world (another passion of mine) or discovering yourself — the greatest adventure of all! Let's start to plant the seed of your adventure, whatever that might be. It may be obvious to you already, but if not, do not worry. By the end of the book you will be clear on which adventure will be your next.

Please note that I refer to 'which adventure' you will pursue, as each adventure will naturally lead to others. For me, Mount Everest will be the ultimate action adventure, but I need to climb a number of mountains first to prepare myself. Now, ironically, Everest is next, and I am prepared; but it has taken me years to get to this point.

So let's start our adventure together where it all began for me … as a child.

Adventurous baby steps: flying the coop

I was raised in a little bungalow nestled between two villages, Llangwm and Hook, in Pembrokeshire, West Wales. I spent most of my childhood playing in the fields, rivers or trees and in the summer down the beach. I look back now and realise how blessed we were. We were happy. We did not need money to be happy… well, maybe 10p for a mixed bag of sweets. But that was just the icing on the cake.

It was amongst this background of the countryside that I got my first taste of adventure, which, according to my mum, really started at one-and-a-half. I was a climber. Not just any climber, but to the point where by the age of two our little bungalow resembled Fort Knox with 5 ft barriers erected all around my garden play area. Unfortunately, for my mother, I am a determined soul, and clearly at this early age a 5 ft barrier wasn't going to deter me. So, at the age of two, I had my first big adventure—I escaped.

My mother recalls me disappearing, having scaled the barriers and taken the dog, Pip, with me. I escaped over the fields that bordered our house. She found my little bobble cap on the barbed wire fence across the nearest fields. (Clearly I was preparing for bad weather even at this age; a lesson I should have taken to Kilimanjaro.) One hour later I was 'captured' by one of the local families. That was one of my first memories because I got a good spanking for it.

But clearly that spanking did not deter me as I topped this feat shortly afterwards by escaping again. This time I managed to get my buggy over the barrier too; I was clearly looking for a faster escape. I was found several hours later, much to the frantic distress of my mother, 2 miles away in the local Hook playing fields. My brother and sister, on the hunt for me, had discovered my buggy in the stream at the bottom of our road. I had used the buggy to go downhill and had abandoned it for the next uphill stretch, using my vehicle choice wisely. I had then summited the steep Furzy Hill on the other side, my first mountain. I should have realised at this early age that it was my destiny to be an adventurer and follow my passions, but it took me many, many more years to do so.

Throughout my youth, I loved the outdoors. Being brought up in beautiful Pembrokeshire was certainly a blessing. I have so many happy memories of exploring new areas of the village and then further afield, playing in the streams and rivers, always having the amazing knack of falling in (much to my mother's distress with her constant washing of my wet and grubby clothes). It was these happy, carefree days that instilled within me my love for nature and the outdoors—a love I would lose for many years during my early adulthood as I became more materialistic and egocentric.

Never ever give up

Besides my Houdini escape routines in those very early years, my childhood generally was nothing exceptional; I did pretty well in school but was very average athletically. At the age of seven, I was hit head-on by a car and broke my femur (thigh bone), which put my average athletic ability back to poor for several years. I remember lying in traction in the hospital bed, with my mother being told that I may not walk properly again. I learnt something that day: *Never listen to what others have to say*. Make your own beliefs. That's what I did, and it was a trait that would reveal itself many times throughout my life. I did walk again, and although I remained very average all through school athletically, I never stopped trying. This would not be the first time I was told I should not or could not do the things by so-called experts, like being told I could never run a marathon by a podiatrist because I am flat-footed… more on that later when I run the toughest footrace on earth.

I was very active in the scouts, and I am sure the people in my village will remember me pottering around with my ex-army gear, Doc Martin boots and Swiss army knife, always prepared for the next adventure and always getting myself into scrapes.

However, my childhood adventuring came to an end when I discovered rugby and girls in my early teens, which was an adventure in itself. And then, of course, there would be the 'wonderful' discovery of alcohol in my late teens. I would not rediscover my passion for adventure for another ten years.

A journey of discovery… re-discovery!

It came as quite a shock when I finally embarked on my journey of self-discovery for the first time in my mid-twenties. I took a good look back over my youth and realised a number of passions I had as a child still remained—my love for nature, adventure, discovery, drawing, reading, painting, gardening and craft—though I wasn't fulfilling any of them.

This book details my rediscovery of my love for action adventure, but I have also simultaneously resurrected several other passions including gardening, reading and drawing. I am sure craft and painting will come a little later in life. It is this balance of life and my passions that keeps me truly fulfilled and happy.

So, what passions from your youth, or indeed adult life, have you left behind, and what could you do now to start living them again? I know you will have plenty of excuses why you do not do them, and we will deal with them in subsequent chapters. For now, just go with the flow. If money and time weren't issues, what would you like to do? I encourage you to have a think about that…

My first marathon

Now let's skip the next few years in my story to my university days. I am sure my adventures with girls, rugby and alcohol is a whole different book with a different title. But it is at this age where I believe we start to lose our innocence, our passion and our truth if we are not careful. We get sent down this system of education and the teenage years are full of peer pressure, groups and conforming. My group was rugby and I behaved accordingly. Now do not get me wrong; I loved these days in a whole different way. But later on in life we sometimes find we are on the wrong path and have forgotten our true path entirely.

So, I no longer delved into the countryside, but more the inside of a bar or club, and I positively frowned upon outdoor recreational sports. I did get a connection pre-university by surfing in Pembrokeshire. I was crap, but carried on anyway. Again, I think this was a longing for the connection to the source, which surfing provides. But choosing a landlocked university at Nottingham curbed this passion.

At university, the household we lived in for the second year was mostly comprised of sports people. There was sporty Luce and Spanner, who were both hockey first team, Colin the medic who was football, and Ed and myself, both rugby union, although I switched codes to league that year. The sixth member of the household, Rachel, was a lovely girl from Hull who wasn't particularly athletic or sporty in any way. After the fresher's fair, she came home to announce she had joined the Rambling Society. Firstly, I needed to get over the shock that there was such a society on the campus, and then I nearly pissed myself laughing at the prospect of a student pottering about, rambling in the moors. Oh, the irony as now there is nothing I love more! So let us learn not to judge, and Rachel, if you are out there... apologies!

Post-university, my ego had developed into the size of a small house, with an air of arrogance. In one interview that I had after I'd finished my degree, the feedback was 'extremely confident, bordering arrogant' which I took as a compliment. Needless to say, I did not get that job. Post-university, rugby, women, materialism and alcohol were still at the top of my adventure agenda, but this was the first real glimpse of feeling that something was missing, a nagging doubt that I did not have it all… although I was trying to kid myself that I did.

My confidence, sometimes blind optimism bordering naivety, would drive me for the next ten years. It was this confidence that got me through challenges early in my life that would seem formidable and unachievable to most people. So, although mine was definitely an over-developed confidence, it is nevertheless an essential trait you need to embark upon your adventure with. It is my intent that your self-esteem will gradually build as you progress through this book. Taking small steps helps build that self-esteem, as you will see in later chapters.

After many years, I have now come to a point in my life where I have found a much better and more fulfilling way to achieve and succeed. You will see this transformation as you progress through the chapters and as you embark upon your own journey and transformation.

If life deals you lemons, make lemonade

Despite the confidence and ego, or perhaps because of it, I had secured a management training job with BOC group, which was a prestigious milk round graduate job, and I was delighted with myself. Then my first role was in sales in Wolverhampton, selling gas to welders. As a chemical engineering graduate fresh from a top university, this was somewhat a kick in the teeth.

Nevertheless, my drive to be the best, which I certainly wasn't at the time, pushed me into a career in sales, and I was determined to make it work.

Now, this was another point in my life where it appeared life has served me lemons, yet with time I produced lemonade. I would never have chosen sales as a profession in a million years. I wanted the nice, plush marketing roles, like my graduate colleagues had down in Guildford. Not trudging around welders' premises getting my nice new suit and fancy shoes dirty. But this role started to teach me to be humble again, to get back to my roots, and slowly I started to lose the edge of arrogance. Unlike most of my fellow graduates, I was from a working class background, so I was able to truly relate to all people, be they a welder, a cleaner or a CEO. This skill was to serve me well.

What had originally appeared as a career setback and an adversity actually led to a long commercial and consulting career, and this grounding in sales was key. I ended up loving my time in Wolverhampton. The group of guys there were excellent and taught me some amazing life lessons in my brief stint there. It also led me back to adventure and my first few challenges, notably the legendary National Three Peaks Challenge, which we will fully discover in Chapter 2. But it really all started with a marathon.

What's my excuse?

It was at this time in my life that a friend and colleague, James Leavesley, challenged me to do a marathon.

I was rubbish at running, but after a few beers and plenty of banter I succumbed, and the next morning, hung over, I signed up. So my future endurance events and adventures were all started as a bet down the pub!

I had signed up for my first marathon, the London Marathon, for the British Heart Foundation, and I had twelve weeks to train. *Plenty of time*, I thought. Now, in these early days this is where ego, drive and naivety won over logic and reality. Thank goodness for naivety, though, as with a lot of adventures, if we really understood what we were letting ourselves in for, we would not try anything in the first place.

At this point in my life, my idea of a run was essentially over 10–20 yards, running at someone on the rugby pitch. Note the 'at', not 'past', as I was a rugby league forward and essentially ran at people. I was fit, but rugby fit, and a 2 mile run was my max. I remember going out for my first 5 mile run eight weeks before the marathon and it nearly killed me.

So let's get into excuses. We all have them, and I had my fair share to rest my laurels on, but I would not let them dictate my future. Over time I have dealt with every single one head-on. Think of your adventure, dreams or goals, and start to think clearly about why you are not doing them—what's your excuse?

After that 5 mile run, I came home with bad asthma and swore to give up. But, then I remembered James Leavesly, and I wasn't going to give him the satisfaction. A strong lesson here is that once you are clear on your goals and your life vision—tell someone. Now let's define that a bit more. Tell someone who will support you, not someone who will mock you. It is amazing how we will let ourselves down consistently, not keeping our promises to ourselves, and yet we will always show up for another whom we respect. If I say I will meet someone down the gym or for a run, I will be there. But if it is just me, it is sometimes so easy to put it off until tomorrow, and tomorrow never comes.

I mentor a number of high performing business people now and have a great coach myself for my endurance events, Stu

Mittleman, and in business I have many. I would never let them down, and neither would my clients let me down.

So, the next day, still sore from my 5 mile run, I went out again. For the following eight weeks I did train, not consistently or in a precise manner, but I did train. The big mistake I made was I just went out and ran, and I kept running until I was knackered. And then I came home. Stupidly, I never measured distance but just made some assumptions based on how fast I thought I was running (which in hindsight was vastly inaccurate). My final assumption was that I had run 18 miles in Scotland on a business trip, so that meant I was ready to go a mere two weeks before the marathon. (I actually measured the distance accurately several years later and it was about 13 miles— which explains my poor performance on the day!)

The day of the marathon came and I was all excited. I stayed in London with my then girlfriend, and the buzz on the morning was infectious. I really do recommend a 5 km, 10 km, half-marathon, marathon or any big event as a goal or indeed a way of life as the energy and buzz on race day is infectious.

The gun went off and we all started running, well walking really, and I spent the next 4 miles in a state of angst and frustration as I could not really get into any form of running or pace as everyone was so packed in. I almost got distracted at the start as the guy next to me, as the gun went off, cracked open a can of lager, said cheers, and offered me one. I respectfully declined. I was in awe of the diversity of people having a go, from old to young, from handicapped to wearing the most ridiculous (and heavy) outfits.

Things started to move after about 4 miles, so I decided to catch up and ran quite well for the next 10 miles.

Then I hit 16 miles (remembering this was already 3 miles past my longest ever distance) and it all went pear shaped. People talk about hitting the wall during marathons. Well, I bounced off it, twice. My legs were in spasm and I had pulled muscles. I had depleted all energy reserves and had nothing left. All in all, the next 8 miles were hell. I remember vividly the stone cobbles by the Tower of London—anyone who has done the London Marathon will know what I am talking about—and each single pebble sent pain ricocheting around my body.

My friends still mock me about this race, as a rhino and a caterpillar allegedly overtook me. That is the wonder of events and endurance races when you look harder.

The heroes and inspiration are all about you. Just take the London Marathon as an example. Could you do it? If not, why not? If one of your goals is a marathon or run of any shape or form, really take a look at your excuses again and then read on.

Who can run the London Marathon? Or to put it another way, who cannot? The oldest person to run the London Marathon is Buster Martin at 101! You have people running it dressed as Santa, people wearing full rhino suits, and the wheelchair event is becoming bigger each year and a true inspiration. You have blind people doing it, people with one leg and even people with or just recovered from cancer. So really, if you want to do it, what's stopping you?

What were my excuses before for not running the London Marathon?

Let's get the common ones out of the way first: I haven't got time; I am so busy with work; I'm just not cut out for running;

I haven't got the right shoes; I can't afford it; What if I fail?; I don't have the energy...

Now, some more challenging ones: I am flat-footed; an asthmatic since childhood, and during winter months and training I get acute asthma; I broke my femur in a car accident when I was seven and essentially had never run more than 2 miles in my life; I was told I was never going to be a runner by my PE teacher; my podiatrist told me I shouldn't run distance; and when measured by a shoe fitter prior to the London Marathon they laughed at me and told me I shouldn't do marathons.

Now I was hardly the candidate to take on six marathons back to back across the Sahara! But then I never really did listen to anyone else unless I believed it myself.

The only things that got me through those miles were pure grit and determination, and a nudge from my ego saying I could not fail. It just wasn't an option, particularly when you are passed by a rhino! For the last 2 miles I had some weird form of second wind, and although painful, I picked myself up—literally—and finished the race. The photo of me finishing has a smile on my face that was masking an underlying grimace.

And this was the beginning of my fascination with endurance and the start of my journey of adventure.

I included this story as I do not want people to think that having done the adventures I have, I am some kind of super-fit, natural runner like Forest Gump; this is far from the truth. I do not pretend to be anything other than average. And I think this story clearly shows that. However, the right preparation, mindset, belief and passion will make a magnificent difference. Also, a sense of reality somewhat in your goals will help you, although that wasn't ever really my forte.

So, from my humble athletic beginnings it is time to start the adventure again and discover mountains for the first time. But before we move to the next chapter, now is the time for you to start your inner-exploration to discover your passions, your goals and dreams, and what adventure of your own I can help you embark on. I suggest you have a journal or a computer document where you record all your answers to the questions in the exploration exercises.

Time for some purposeful exploration!

Purpose and Passion

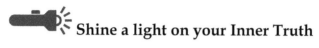 **Shine a light on your Inner Truth**

Ask yourself the following questions:

- If you did not have to work, what would you fill your day doing? How would that feel?

- If you volunteered for an organisation, industry or movement, what would it be? Why don't you do it now?

- What are you passionate about? When you think of this, how does it make you feel?

- If you watch a film or read a book, what scenes always raise your emotions? (Crying, laughing, compassion, etc.)

- Did any common themes with your passions emerge from answering the questions in this section? Write these down as these feelings leave a breadcrumb trail of clues to your true passions.

Map out your True Path

- What great adventures or passions would you like to explore in life? (Remember, this is not necessarily about action adventures.)

- Which adventure/passion in life would you like to pursue next?

- Childhood dreams:
    - What did you want to be when you grew up?
    - What did you love to do as a child?

- – If you could go back now for a day, what would you do?
- What do you love or wish you could do now?
- Based on your answers to the above questions, what do you see as your over-riding passion(s)?

📖 Let your True Guide lead the way

Looking back over your life, think of a time when you faced a hardship, a challenge, a massive setback or a trauma and how devastating it felt at the time.

- Now reflect on how you overcame it, if it has served you, how something unexpected has come from that time, perhaps something good. You might not be able to see it yet as maybe the magic has not unfolded fully. So, if not, look back further and explore another situation. Write down your reflections.
- List 5 personal successes/achievements since you were born
- List 5 talents/skills that have resulted from the above experiences

The beliefs I am encouraging you to start to imprint here are:

- Everything happens for a reason
- Everything is in perfect time
- Magic happens around you every day
- God is good…. whatever god that may be to you.
- Start to believe this, even a tiny bit, and we are off to a flying start!

Identify your inner True North

- Choose one of your adventures/dreams/ goals/aspirations. What are your excuses for not achieving it already or for not trying it now?

- Take those excuses and give several good reasons why they are all bull. Now it is time to step up and claim your true destiny.

- Write a movie script for YOUR PERFECT DAY. Describe it in as much detail as possible, from the moment you wake up, where you are, who's there, what you do for the day — involve all your senses and emotions so it feels real. Do not limit yourself and just write.

- Now what can you do today to make today just that little bit more perfect?

Chapter 2

The National Three Peaks Challenge

BUILDING BELIEF AND VISION

First say to yourself what you would be;
and then do what you have to do.
~ Epictetus

"The Russian guide came up to me, looking troubled, and in broken English he said we needed to make a decision. He had been on the satellite phone downstairs, checking on the weather patterns, and debating for some time now with other guides. The weather was bad, had been bad, and was likely to continue to be bad. But there was a slights chance we could give the summit a shot. If we did not try, we may not get another chance…

Given my experience on Kilimanjaro, I knew I wasn't acclimatized and did not want to screw another summit up. To add fuel to the fire, this was a very dangerous gamble because if the weather did come down on me anywhere near the ferocity raging outside whilst I had altitude issues, the combination could be fatal."

Believe first and foremost in yourself

Most people do not have any clue on their passions, or if they do, they are doing their very best in ignoring them—distracting themselves with work, TV, computer games or whatever else the Western world has come up with to distract us from our true passions. Those insightful few, however, who do recognise or embrace their passion, which could be you now, can often stumble on the next key stage of the adventure.

This is belief in yourself, otherwise translated into 'self-esteem' or 'confidence'.

If you have been side-stepping your passions until now, hopefully by going through Chapter 1 you have started to identify your passions (though I suggest that you just begin with one). It may be vague at this point, which is just fine, or indeed crystal clear. Either way, the seeds have now been sown. With a passion and purpose identified, and also some initial excuses eradicated or at least challenged, we will now build upon this initial concept of passion and, more importantly, start to move on to this next key stage— belief . This is the point where the rubber hits the road.

So, I want to be an adventurer, I want to climb mountains, I am passionate and I have no excuses left. What now? Well, perhaps I am not made to do it. Perhaps it's just not for me. Perhaps I am not good enough. Perhaps I will fail … But perhaps, just perhaps, I will succeed.

Keep your dreams and visions alive

Not to have dreams, goals and adventures is one thing, but to have them and not believe you can achieve them, that is entirely another story and a very sad one. I find this is the saddest point in the lives of people I meet and where I see most dreams die. I have witnessed this so many times, people in awe of my adventure success, the Marathon des Sables in particular, saying how they wish they could do something like that, but they just cannot. I always respond with "Why not?" And I have not heard one decent response yet.

So, you have to believe, first and foremost, in you.

The human being, aka YOU, is just incredible. You are unique, and your body and mind are part of one of the most amazing systems in the universe. Whatever it is that another human being has achieved, you have the power to do likewise. In fact you have the power to do things that only you can conceive and perhaps nobody else has dared — you are powerful beyond measure.

A little confidence, a little self-esteem to start with, will build and grow as you pursue your journey of adventure. That is part of the magic as it is self- perpetuating. You start small and with each success (or failure) you grow in confidence slowly but surely — like I did. I started with a 2 mile run and years later I was doing the Marathon des Sables in confidence. I started with a small hill and my goal is to end up on top of Everest. But confidence builds slowly, and it takes time and patience to nurture it. There is no better time than now to start this process.

We will discuss vision more fully later, but I just want to make an important point on vision and belief.

Sometimes people can have great big visions, so big that they do not actually believe in them as the mountain seems too high to climb. Hence, they get disillusioned and they give up early, if indeed try at all. I have seen this in a number of clients of mine who came to me with incredible visions of wealth and prosperity whilst being in a position of near bankruptcy. Whilst the vision is admirable, when it is so far removed from the here and now, it can have a negative effect. So what I would encourage you to do is have *sub-visions*. Keep the grand vision, always keep the grand vision, but break it down to a more realistic vision that will appear a lot closer and, most importantly, you truly believe in.

Everest is like this for me. The cost, the time, the risk, the technical ability and the fitness are all quite overpowering, and it is easy to not believe I can do it. But I do believe, maybe not for today or next year, or even the year after, but some day. In the meantime, I will build my skills, slowly starting with much smaller mountains, mountains I do believe I can do. And my confidence will build, slowly but surely.

Creating the right timeline for you

I want to talk about timelines briefly as they are really quite key to having a vision. Timelines are concepts used in NLP (Neuro-Linguistic Programming) that help in goal-setting, visions and coaching. Everyone has a timeline and each person's is very different; this never ceases to amaze me. Essentially, everyone either has dominant thoughts focussed on the past, present or future. How close these are to you and your day-to-day consciousness very much depends on your timeline.

This is powerful stuff, so stick with me on this and try the action at the end of the chapter. If you find it really interests you, I encourage you to seek out a coach.

Let me get to my main point by sharing some examples of how we can visualise and map out our timeline. I view my timeline as a line going straight behind me and straight ahead of me. I have trouble remembering details of the past as it is so far behind me. The present is right in my lap, and I can quite easily map out one to two years ahead as being right in front of my vision within a few meters. After three years, the line is getting hazy and moving into the distance. I therefore set my dominant visions one year ahead in detail whilst holding an overarching, more general vision on life for three to five years.

A close friend, however, lives much more in the past, with most past memories being very close to her shoulder. Hence, she dwells on the past a lot, but is also very much in the moment. She struggles massively with future planning—one month is out of the room to her and three months plus is on the horizon. So mapping a life vision is going to be much tougher for her. But she is an Accident and Emergency doctor, and an amazing one, so where do you want her timeline to be?

(Also, as an aside, it is worth noting the possible effects on relationships with each partner having very different modalities. Without understanding, these can lead to significant friction. The great adventure of love, however, is a whole different book.)

I have had clients whose whole past sits on their shoulders, some who could map twenty years in the room, and some who could not see past tomorrow. So, do not panic if you struggle to see clearly into the future. Choose whatever timeline suits you and you feel comfortable with. If you wish to explore further or want help with your timeline, then seek out an NLP coach. Try to get some clear perspective on your timeline as this will really affect how far ahead you set your vision, how you take action and whether or not you need to deal more with the past and clear more excuses and fears. (Note: I am not a coach. But if you contact me at DiamondLifeDesign.com and we can help you find one.)

What about if you are already confident and have strong self-esteem? Then great, just like in my case, this is not a weakness. But also learn to harness it. The following story will elaborate on how confidence can get you through despite naivety. Confidence is one trait, but a clear vision, direction and planning is also important. We will cover these in the next chapters.

The Three Peaks Challenge - the adventure begins

Following the London Marathon, I had the bug for events and challenge. The next one that I was challenged with, again somewhat reactively, was the National Three Peaks challenge. I was settling in nicely with BOC Group and had quite a social scene with most of the staff, which is where I heard of this challenge for the first time. Again, it was a challenge thrown down in the pub by some of the guys who were working in the bottling plant in Wolverhampton. Out one night in Wolves, one of the guys I worked with starting talking about pulling a team together to do the Three Peaks, which was the first time I had heard of the challenge. Again, confidence and naivety, led by ego, drove my emotions so I signed up! I was pretty fresh from the London Marathon and playing rugby for the Dudley Kings in Kingswinford, Birmingham, so I was relatively fit and felt up for the challenge.

The Three Peaks is an infamous endurance event for the budding mountaineer-come-endurance athlete, and it is more accessible than most of the international challenges and one that will stay with me for a lifetime. It is essentially a race against time, a logistical challenge, as well as an obvious physical challenge.

You have to climb the three highest peaks in the British Isles, starting in Scotland with Ben Nevis, 1,344 m, then Scafell Pike in the Lake District, England at 978 m and finishing in my homeland, Wales, with Snowdon in Snowdonia National Park, one of my favourite mountains at 1,085 m. Over 3,000 m of climbing in total. To put that in perspective, that's the equivalent of half of Kilimanjaro in 24 hours.

This is no small feat in its own right as each is a challenging peak. It doesn't require real climbing or mountaineering per se, but is more a very challenging trek. Now put all three together and the crux of the challenge is you need to do all three in 24 hours! Again, challenging enough, but all three are geographically dispersed with one in each country. The driving time between them all is about ten to twelve hours, not leaving much room for error or complacency on the mountain.

So, there was the challenge laid out for me. Just like in my first foray into adventure with the marathon, I had no experience, no specific training and very little time to prepare. My idea of a mountain was the hill rambling I had done as a child with my parents in the Preseli Hills (sometimes called Preseli Mountains) in Pembrokeshire. These rise to a lofty height of 540m, and I think you must start climbing at about 300 – 400m. In hindsight, my idea of a climb was a mere few hundred meters, and I had just signed up to climb 3,000 m plus in 24 hours. Thank goodness I was naive enough not to realise this at the time or I may never have started.

So, having my false illusion of the Preseli 'Mountains' in my head as a benchmark, I was relatively comfortable and confident. Wrong benchmark! At this point in my life, I did not realise that I had never really seen a real mountain in my life, only on TV where they look small compared to the brutal reality. In hindsight, the Preseli Mountains are mere hillocks, a dot on the landscape compared to the big summits yet to come.

But I did not know any better, which was probably just as well.

As I was playing rugby at the time and working hard in my new role, I had no time for any specific training, so I just carried on business as usual with the confidence my fitness would see me through. How hard could it be anyway?

Six weeks from the big event, the team was fully formed and we all met around the leader's house for a briefing. It was a real mix of people: two guys in their late twenties from the bottling plant who were very outdoors-oriented, Schneider and Lickit, being part of the army volunteers; two older guys who were experienced ramblers-come orienteers (one was the leader and in his 50's); another colleague, Mark, my age, who was in his early twenties and more experienced in orienteering and trekking; and then there was me, zero experience but keen. They were a really good set of people and we all got on great, so what could go wrong?

My first real mountain, the fast way

Four weeks out, we went on the first (and last) trial climb on Snowdon. It was a beautiful day and we went up the Pyg Track[2]. I was in awe of the beauty, the magnificence and the size of Snowdon, still one of my favourite peaks to this day. I was also starting to have an idea of what I had got myself into, although

---

[2] The Pyg track is the shortest way up Snowdon, but the steepest, and involves the least amount of ascent. It is 5.5 km in length and involves around 800 m of ascent.

still not fully comprehending that this was the smallest of the peaks.

We took our time going up to the top, but on the way down Schneider introduced me to a running descent, and we ran all the way down. This is still my favourite form of descent and a method I would use on many peaks, including Kilimanjaro. I find it a lot easier on the toes and so exhilarating it keeps the mind alert and the adrenalin pumping on what can be a boring descent. Highly dangerous, though. This specific descent still remains as one of my all-time bests in speed and exhilaration. Once we got going, we could not stop, and halfway down at full speed I missed a turn and went careering over the side of the mountain, the closest I have felt like flying, even compared to skydiving. I flew through the air before hitting a huge scree slope, which I slid down for 200 ft. I got to the bottom, bounced up and carried on running as if it was all planned! I remember the look on some ramblers' faces at the bottom who had witnessed it all. Their looks said: "You are bloody mad!" This tactic, however, would prove critical in the upcoming Three Peaks, but is not one I encourage. If that scree slope had not been there, I might not be writing this book right now.

All in all, this first day on the mountain was wonderful, but I was yet to fully realise the passion that fuelled me. Ultimately, it was this first mountain that would spur my future quest for the Seven Summits. Every huge vision starts in humble beginnings.

Although I felt pretty good on the mountain and my fitness held up well, the next day I hurt like hell and could hardly move, as of course I was using muscles I had not used before. Anyway, the test run was done and all that was needed now was the big day itself, starting off with Ben Nevis.

A long way to Scotland

The team leader had got hold of the company minibus and a driver. We also had the Operations Director who came to jolly us along and was also responsible for the food to fuel us in between peaks. The night before the climb, we drove all the way to Fort William, Scotland, where we were to begin this epic adventure. At this point in my life I wasn't very well travelled, so I really could not get over how far away Scotland was. It looked quite close on the map.

It was here we had our kit check, to which I realised I was wholly unprepared. Looking back now, I cringe. I was the person you hear about on the news. Going into the mountains of Scotland and having to be rescued in appalling conditions as they are wearing shorts and T-shirt with a Snickers bar as backup. I did indeed have shorts, as that's all I ever trained for rugby in, trainers (no boots), some T-shirts and a fleece top. I had two flimsy waterproofs that were worn on the sidelines for rugby, definitely not built for mountains, and, as I was soon to discover, were not waterproof either. The leader, realising my inadequacy, sent me off shopping, and the team cobbled together a spare pair of boots and a pack; I did not even have a backpack! I had pockets, so what did I need a pack for?

The kit I have now, and the respect I have for even the smallest peaks in the Black Mountains of Wales, is a world apart from these naive beginnings. You never see me now without water, food, compass or medical supplies; these early days were to teach me some valuable lessons. I was the brunt of many jokes that first evening and ridiculed by the mountaineering community, all of which I took in my stride and used to fuel me in the 24 hours to come as I set out to prove to everyone that there was more to climbing than fancy kit and snazzy boots. And maybe, I was hoping, I was to have the last laugh after all.

Ben Nevis is a bit of a blur to me; I just remember grey and wet. It was a beast of a mountain from the very beginning when we started off in the afternoon on a miserable, wet and very cold day. I do remember false summit after false summit all the way up as I had no concept of its size. I kept thinking the top could not be far now, only to go another hour and still be no closer. The cold on that mountain, with my inadequate kit, cut through to the bone — a chill I will never forget. I spent the whole afternoon just trying to keep warm. The summit was a sombre affair with a quick snapshot and swift retreat.

I cannot remember exactly, but we must have been a good five to six hours in that cold misery. Because of our late start, it was nightfall by the time we returned to the bus, and I was never happier than when I could see the lights in Fort William on our descent.

In the final hour of descent, all any of us thought about was the hot food and hot drink that would be awaiting our return. On getting to the bus, however, our colleagues announced the cooker had broken. Nothing was open, so we would have to do with some day-old sandwiches that they had drummed up locally. Not the most motivating of welcomes.

I was soaking wet (as my so-called waterproofs really weren't waterproof at all), cold to the bone, starving hungry and knackered as I had just climbed the biggest thing I had ever seen or imagined. Now I knew why the Scots are so tough. I stripped off my layers in the minibus, hung my clothes around the bus to try to dry them (as I did not have any spare) and curled up in a ball on the back seat to attempt some fitful sleeping on the way to Scafell. This is where, whilst in slumber and unbeknown to me, logistics started to go pear-shaped.

We had stopped at a service station part way down to fuel up, but there was still only cold food as it was the middle of the night and nothing was open. Then some six hours after leaving Fort William, we were getting close to Scafell and everyone was getting their kit together. I squirreled around to retrieve my drying clothes. They were still cold and damp, and I shivered feverishly as I pulled each layer back onto my damp body, piece by piece. To add fuel to the fire (or ice for that matter), it was the middle of the night and bloody cold outside. Just as well I had another T-shirt to add on! My belief was starting to waver as I started to realise my inadequacies and the stupidity of my kit.

A cold, dark night - lost on Scafell

There was a lot of arguing in the front of the bus. It soon became evident that we were a little lost in the middle of the Lake District, in the middle of the night, a time long before satellite navigation (sat nav). We finally pulled up at the starting place, and into the night we all trekked, cold, de-motivated and miserable in the pitch black. Surprise, surprise… I did not have a torch with me! So, I had to focus keenly in the gloom ahead to follow the beams of my peers and stop myself from tripping on the rubble path. A very painful process that lasted for hours.

Many hours later, just as the sun was attempting some form of rise through the gloom, the team fell apart.

The younger guys had been constantly ahead whilst I lingered at the back with the two older guys whose pace was a lot slower. I was to learn a very valuable lesson that night back there with the older guys: *The team is only as fast as the slowest man.* A good metaphor on life.

There was disagreement about the routes to take, and it was evident that we were lost. The two older guys had had enough, and after a heated exchange of words, they decided to head back, leaving the four of us young guns sitting on the mountain.

The other three argued for a while then we headed off in some form of direction. An hour later, it appeared we were still lost and another argument broke out. I just sat back and observed all this. As a novice on the mountain, I had no opinion and no right to an opinion really. But my natural leadership instinct was starting to get irritated, and whilst they were all arguing I heard something. It was like a sixth instinct, and to this day I still do not know what I heard. But every sense in my body was telling me to follow it. So I did. I told the others I heard something and to follow me.

At first they ignored me, still in full fight-mode, so I just went anyway and disappeared over the ridge.

After a while, they all clambered after me. Five minutes later, we hit a main path, saw some spotlights and heard some voices; we had hit the main trail and were nearly at the top! Hallelujah!

This just goes to show how sometimes you can be so close to something, so near to your vision or your goal, and you just need to have a little faith, follow your instincts or just hang in there. We could have so easily given up just moments before, and we would never have known how close we were. Such is life.

We summited for a brief moment, turned around and got down as quickly as possible. As it turns out, we had parked in totally the wrong spot and climbed up the wrong side of the mountain!

All the arguing was because all the trails were new and the old heads that had done it before must have been confused in the night. But we had done it, and we were down. Still no hot food, but I was starting to dry out at least as the sun had come out. Provided we had a good run to Snowdonia, we still had a slight chance of reaching our goal.

Doing the impossible

But… we did not have a good run to Snowdonia. We had a terrible run. We stopped for hot food, which wasted precious time, and then we hit a carnival in one of the towns in North Wales where the roads were shut, and it delayed us by two hours. The driver nearly turned around there and then, but we all insisted we crack on as precious time was running out.

We were all now totally exhausted … and getting sore. It usually take 24 hours for me to get really sore after gym workouts or rugby matches, and bang on schedule my body was now getting very sore and stiff. Motivation was at an all-time low.

We reached Snowdon two hours before the 24-hour deadline. It had taken us three-and-a-half hours in our test run, and that was when we were fresh. Now we had two mountains in our legs and a few hours of fitful sleep. *It's impossible.* I still hear those words now.

The two older guys who had already dropped out told us quite bluntly it was impossible, and given their vast experience who was I to argue? Then something magical happened.

Just when motivation could not go any lower, the Operations Director turned to me and winked. This was a man who I had huge respect for and truly liked. He said very matter-of-factly, "Well, if anyone can do this, Deri can." Those few words of encouragement lit a fire inside me in an instant; **someone believed in me**… even though I did not believe in myself. The day had turned out quite nice and the sun was shining. I took off all my wet kit and put on my shorts, T-shirt and a pair of trainers. My naivety in kit was about to pay off.

The bus was nearly there and my adrenalin was pumping. We knew the only way to do this was to run it. So as soon as the bus stopped, the four of us were out and bounding up the mountain. Within thirty minutes there was a clash of opinions between me, Lickit and the other two. (You'll soon find out how Lickit got his unusual nickname). They wanted to take a different trail, and given they were the experienced ones I really should have listened. But my gut and sixth sense was now screaming at me and telling me "No", and so I followed it, and Lickit followed me.

I took what looked like a tough trail, but a direct one — definitely the road less travelled. And so there we were, Lickit and I, alone. Now there were two. We were still running.

Halfway up, I was totally out of gas, no reserves, nothing, and Lickit started leading the way. I stopped to take a breath. My lungs were screaming at me to give up. It would have been so easy to do as we were trying the impossible; no one would blame us. But thankfully Lickit was now so pumped and motivated he was unstoppable. I got carried along by his enthusiasm and encouragement. I found my second wind and tapped into an energy of the mountain and of myself that was deeper than anything I'd ever known.

Onwards, upwards. It got gloomier, cloudier and wetter as we went into and then above the clouds. We kept on battling, and then out of nowhere was the summit! Without even taking time to savour the moment, we touched the summit point, high-fived and turned around and just ran. Lickit was shouting "Lick it!" all the way down, hence his name. We ran all the way down, careering, letting gravity take us in its embrace as we had nothing left in our own tanks. It felt like we were just falling all the way. It was totally liberating. We ran our last few steps over the finish line with our comrades cheering and whooping for joy. We had done it in 23 hours, 58 minutes and 30 seconds— divine timing. One slip, one tumble, one more traffic light and it would have been all over. That day I built belief in myself. If I could do that, then I could do anything. It set me up for future adventures and the realisation that when the going gets tough, the human body is an amazingly resilient thing. It was not only the belief in myself, though, that had spurred me on. The belief the Operations Director had in me had been infectious, and it was his words that truly ignited me. And then when I could have given up, it was my teammate Lickit who pulled me through and encouraged me.

So surround yourself with people who have belief in you and will support you. And be that belief, also, for other people; your impact can be profound. I thank my old BOC team because in that moment a seed of a big vision was born. A vision of the Seven Summits and climbing the highest mountains on earth.

Despite this wonderful experience, I did not climb another peak for another ten years as I got wrapped up in the corporate world and the rat race, and I would have to rediscover my passion all over again. You have to hold your passion and your beliefs closely to you and nurture them as they can disappear in an instant.

The next adventure would be a long way off, on the other side of the world, a world away from Wales.

Time for some self-belief exercises!

TRUE Thinking on

BELIEFS AND VALUES

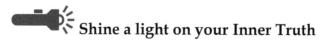 **Shine a light on your Inner Truth**

Take a moment to think of your adventure or goal. What good feelings well up inside you? Excitement, passion, curiosity, intrigue, joy? Really feel them, list them and focus on feeling and connecting to them throughout the journey. Try to live like this every day.

- Were there any negative feelings that you were feeling? Fear, uncertainty, overwhelm? List these, too, and really look at them deeply to see if they are real or just excuses. We will deal with fear in a later chapter.

Map out your True Path

Think through what you have achieved in life so far; you may surprise yourself. From learning to walk, to your first swim badge, to passing any form of exam, to your first girlfriend/ boyfriend … These are all accomplishments.

Go really deep. Start to understand how great you already are. Go through ages 1-5, 6-12, 13- 18, 19-30, 31-40, 41-50 and so on, and find at least three successes per age category.

- Acknowledge your achievements and commit to build upon them.

- Now think about your passions or adventure. Choose someone you admire, someone who has achieved what you want to achieve and study them diligently. Maybe, just maybe, they were like you once. So, what's stopping you? Write down all their character traits and seek to become a little more like them every day.

Let your True Guide lead the way

- What little steps can you take right now to build your confidence towards your passion and adventure? What will give you a little confidence and belief? Who can give you that pep talk? Whatever it is, whoever it is, do it now, whether it's having on hand some inspirational CD's, DVD's or book or joining your local trekking club to build up your confidence.

  Choose someone who will support you — a coach or mentor. It doesn't have to be a formal arrangement, although I highly rate it. It could be a good friend or family member. Choose an encouraging person who will also hold you accountable, someone who will believe in you when even you do not.

- Be the spark of belief for other people; do it today!

Identify your inner True North

- Start to listen to or feel your sixth sense or intuition — what your gut is telling you. If you get these feelings or inklings, write them down, and then see what happens when you either go with them or go against them. I have learnt the hard way that my gut is always right, but it has taken me years to tune into it.

- Write down and start to repeat daily affirmations — positive statements of reinforcement to encourage you in your quest. They must be positive, for example, not "I don't want to be fat" rather "I am feeling increasingly slimmer and healthier every day". These may feel awkward at first and your belief may be low, but stick with it. Ensure you are taking action every day and feel your way forward in the belief.

Chapter 3

Kosciuszko, A New Start Down Under

THE LESSON LEARNT

Life isn't about finding yourself.
Life is about creating yourself.
~ George Bernard Shaw

"I was now the highest I had ever been by a long way, way higher even than the dizzy heights of Kilimanjaro, each step a new adventure into the unknown. The high altitude was taking its toll as each step seemed to get slower and slower, and each breath deeper and deeper to get me the same amount of oxygen relief.

As we approached the ridge of the next key milestone, Independencia at 20, 790 ft, I glanced upwards for the first time in thirty minutes, as I had only been focused on my feet. As I looked towards what must be Independencia, I stopped instantly and gasped, not for air but in awe at what I saw. Was it a vision? Was it real? Or was I going mad? ... Even with the effects of altitude, it shocked me so much I stumbled and fell to one knee.

There I was, on the heights of the Aconcagua, the highest point I had ever reached, on one knee in front of..."

Rediscovering my Passion

Following the Three Peaks Challenge and the London Marathon, I rested on my laurels for many years. I became immersed in my work and my own perceived success. As my business success built, so did my income and with it my ego and levels of extravagance. I drank champagne like it was pop and ate in the finest restaurants. As a top sales executive in the city, I was on full first-class expenses, of which client entertainment was a big part. This added further fuel to the fire.

This was a time of excess, massive excess. By my mid- twenties, I was earning a six-figure salary and living life and its excesses to the max. I was drinking most nights of the week with clients and colleagues, living near York in the west wing of a hall, commuting first class to London and living out of fine hotels most of the week. A wonderful life some may think! I certainly could not complain. But believe me when I say that it is nice for a while, and then slowly you start losing your health and with it your soul.

During this period, my fitness became less and less, to the point of hardly anything at all. I still talked about the Three Peaks, the Marathon and my rugby as if I were still that fit person and making excuses for why I wasn't currently doing anything: injury, work, business ... all weak, directionless excuses. I talked about my dreams of the Marathon des Sables and the big mountains, but all this was so far removed from my own reality, physically and mentally, it was mere hot air. My confidence and bravado were masking an underlying disbelief and incongruence in my life; confidence and delusion are a fine line indeed. And although I had a vague vision of where I wanted to go, I wasn't moving towards it, rather far from it; I was moving away.

Sometimes in life you need to hit breaking point in order to change direction. Sometimes the Universe/God will take significant action to boot you back on your true life's course, which at the time may feel like adversity (There's that word again). Having a passion you are following, an unwavering belief in yourself and a bigger vision of what can be and what you are capable of, are what can help get you through these adversities.

So, what we need to build next is the **vision.**

Building the vision

At the very peak of my business performance, earning a huge wage and living life to excess, several things happened at once. I got increasingly ill to the point where I had to have a colonoscopy as my excessive lifestyle had finally caught up with me. And the day after the infamous September 11, I was put on redeployment, which is a posh word for redundancy. Suddenly the world collapses around you, literally.

Thankfully, I had a wonderful girlfriend who put up with all my issues and was there for me when I needed her the most. *I will come back to love in the final chapter, so I won't spoil the fun here.* I suddenly had precious time to myself on three months of 'gardening leave' — but no garden — to reflect on life and what I had become. The problem was what I saw I did not like. So I took an extreme measure and decided to take extended time to reflect on myself and what I wanted in life. I decided to do an MBA, not just anywhere, but with the number one school in Australasia, AGSM[3], Sydney, Australia — the other side of

---

[3] Australian Graduate School of Management, Sydney

the world. I needed to get as far away as I could from my current lifestyle and excesses before I destroyed myself.

So, after a gruelling application process and entrance exams, I scraped in. I sold everything I owned, my plush house (part of a Georgian manor), my BMW Z3 and all my expensive possessions. I gave all my furniture and household things to my girlfriend, packed up two big boxes and went to Australia. After a time of reflection, I went a bit wild in my first few months in Sydney. But despite this, I entered into a real space of self-discovery that would change my life forever.

Sometimes you need to take time out, time to reflect, to rediscover yourself, to rebuild yourself, and this is what Sydney did for me. I worked hard and played hard in Sydney, but I did reconnect to nature and my fitness. In the sunshine and beaches, it is hard not to want to go for a run or a swim. So, slowly I rebuilt myself from the ground up.

It was during this period that I started to play rugby again, although way below my previous form, which was highly frustrating. Nevertheless, I enjoyed my season … little knowing it would be my last. My final game was playing in the MBA World Championships in North Carolina, USA, against Harvard in the quarter finals. We won, and I was smashed … And so endeth my rugby career. I was essentially spear tackled off the ball by three very large American football players from three different angles. Ouch! I was stretchered off the field and taken by ambulance to the hospital where, before entry, I remember having to prove I had medical insurance and sign my life away. Thank goodness for the National Health Service in the UK; we should all be eternally grateful.

Following CT scans, X-rays and tests, it was confirmed that I had bruising on the brain and ripped muscles down each side of my spine. I could not move and was in agony. That was definitely the end of my rugby career and of my fitness for a while. The excuses kicked in proper now. I had legitimate injury, so I could be excused from not achieving anything more 'sporty' in my life. I hear so many people speak of how sporty they were when young, but they then got an injury and so *cannot* do anything anymore. And nearly every time it is total bull.

I know this because I used these excuses too. But, after six months of recovery, I knew I needed to get fit and have a focus. It was time to ditch the excuses and reconnect with the outdoors. I spent many weekends out trekking (or, as the Aussies say, bushwalking) in the bush with friends, running along the coasts around Sydney and taking camping trips in the Blue or Snowy Mountains. It was a magical time and Australia is a truly magical place. This experience was enough for me to commit to a lifetime of outdoors and adventure and is where my passion for adventure was truly reborn.

I had **passion,** which was certain now, and **belief** in myself and my abilities. Now I needed a **vision.** A number of things helped me consolidate my vision over several years in all areas of my life, but probably the most intense experience was whilst participating in a week-long seminar on the Gold Coast, Australia, with Tony Robbins. For those who do not know Tony Robbins, he is a global motivational speaker and leader. Post-Australia, I committed to doing his *Mastery University* set of seminars. The seminar that I attended on the Gold Coast was called *Date with Destiny*, and amongst many lessons and learnings, it really helps hone your passion, purpose and vision in life.

It was here that I ultimately committed to my adventure and to this book, although I did not take action on the book for some years. The next few years would prove an incredible adventure journey. One of the key lessons I took away from Tony's seminar, which I may add is a cross between a pop concert and a week-long intense version of Oprah Winfrey, was what Tony calls the 'Six Human Needs'. I am not sure where this concept originates, so I can only presume it is from Tony himself.

The basic theme is that despite all our differences, all humans the world over have a clearly defined set of core needs: the Six Human Needs.

The first two are **Certainty** and **Variety**, a paradox which we all face.

Then we have **Significance** and **Love/Connection**, another paradox.

Finally, **Growth** and **Contribution.**

Hit four to five of these needs with an activity, goal or passion and you have an addiction, which can be good or bad.

Let us take an alcoholic as an example. You get **certainty** from the drink: you know what it feels like and that it will feel good in the moment. With that feeling then comes **variety** as each session is different and brings different things, people and sensations. A 2-needs hit. Whilst you are drinking, the alcohol gives you your own sense of **significance** and so self-esteem usually builds (Dutch courage). With that comes a sense of **connection** to the alcohol and to others as you let a lot of inhibitions go. A 4-needs hit and you have a habit or addiction. The sad thing is the two most important needs of all rarely get touched in a bad habit, with no sense of contribution and no growth of 'your- self'. In fact you are on a negative decline.

Now let us look at a positive example, like adventure. For me, adventure has **certainty.** I *know* I will love it; it will feel great and I will be in nature, witnessing some amazing sights. With that also comes a lot of **uncertainty** from the possible **varieties** of experiences — I won't know what it will feel like, look like, how the high altitude will affect me, what the weather will throw at me and so on. Clearly a 2-needs hit. Doing adventure definitely gives you a sense of **significance** to yourself and others. You just know you are doing some amazing feats that many people have not done, and that makes you a little unique.

Connection, yes, absolutely, first and foremost with yourself, with spirit and with the people around you with whom you bond in a deep and profound way through the extremeness of what you are undertaking together. A 4-need hit.

Adventure brings **growth** physically with training for the events, and it brings internal growth and increased self-esteem through the learning and lessons in the experience. A 5-need hit.

Finally, **contribution.** Well, if five hits are not enough already to ingrain a solid addiction then adding contribution to the mix kind of seals the deal that adventure is a healthy addiction that touches all six types of human needs. Sharing my stories and motivation in this book and on the web and helping inspire people through talks and personal sessions, and doing the big events for various charities, are all my contribution.

By now I hope you get a feel for the power of the Six Human Needs (Tony teaches this way better than I ever could). Now, why is this so important? Well, if you have a passion, a belief and a vision but only two or three of your needs are met in the process, you are unlikely to follow through and be motivated … and I would question if it is indeed a passion or a whim. So, this is a great test for your passion to ensure you have the intrinsic motivation for the next steps. We will do a proper exercise on this at the end of the chapter. If you are finding only a few are being fulfilled, then think what you can do to add to the others, or consider if the adventure is really what you want to do at all.

This is also a very powerful tool for relationships because if your relationship doesn't meet at least four basic needs, then you are on a slippery slope. But, as I keep saying, love is a lesson for another book. (*Love's Great Adventure!* I really must write that).

By the time I left *Date with Destiny,* I had a clear vision for my life in all areas, with adventure being right up there near the top. (My family and health will always come first.) My new vision for my life's great adventure was to complete the Global Grand Slam—a term I think I saw somewhere once but have now made it uniquely mine. This encompassed the greatest adventures on earth: The Seven Summits (The highest mountain on each continent culminating in Everest), the North and South Poles, the Marathon des Sables, the Jungle Marathon and an Ironman, all of which would keep me busy for many years. You just know when you have hit a passion head-on when just thinking about it and how you will achieve it makes you want to explode with excitement whilst simultaneously being slightly scared and daunted.

Where on earth do you start with such a vision? *One step at a time, the smallest one first.* And there is no time like the present. So, for me that meant flying from Brisbane to Canberra straight from the course to take on Mount KosciuszKo with my old bushwalker pal, Hamish Black. We were to do some trekking down the Snowy River and while there I could attempt the first of the Seven Summits, Mount KosciuszKo in the Snowy Mountains.

Like all great adventures, it starts small and builds. KosciuszKo is a small but picturesque peak standing at the top of the Snowy Mountains in south-east Australia. Late one morning, we arrived in the Thredbo district to a beautiful mountain scene. I had actually been here some years before on the British Lions rugby tour, but it was in winter when it is a ski resort (Yes, a ski resort in Australia!). But now it was summer and the beauty was just breathtaking. We parked Hamish's old Jeep, got a few last provisions from the shop (Yes, I learned from my Three Summit experience!) and headed up the mountain.

I cannot say it was very difficult. In fact it was a piece of cake as we took a nice easy trek up to the summit from Thredbo. Being summer, the ground was clear, the sun was out and we had glorious views across the Snowy Mountains. We peaked quite late in the afternoon, and for the first time I took precious moments to savour the experience. Unfortunately, it wasn't the serene picture I was hoping for as some TV footage was being filmed and there were a lot of cameras around, which we did our best to get in front of, unsuccessfully.

After our descent, we headed deeper into the Snowy Mountains to camp for the night, exhilarated that the first of the Seven Peaks was bagged. Boy, it felt great. *How hard could this be?* Little did I know just what a walk in the park this would be compared to the rest. Yet this little adventure was far from over and had its own test to come.

We put up the tent in the middle of nowhere and gathered wood for a fire to warm us. As we settled in, we watched the most magnificent sunset, and I just knew I was in heaven itself. The serenity was smashed a moment later as no sooner had the sun dropped below the horizon, the temperature plummeted with her. It was suddenly freezing. Now, I thought I had come prepared with a spare kit and sleeping bag, but nothing prepared me for the cold that night. Hamish poked fun at me most of the evening at how soft I was as I sat there shivering. The one consolation was gazing up at the star-filled sky, which was breathtaking, as I shivered myself to sleep.

The next day was magnificent as we trekked deeper and deeper into the Snowy Mountains and bagged a number of peaks on the way, getting more and more remote. Soon there were no trails at all. We now had to cut our way through the undergrowth and fight through dense foliage. I finally felt like an explorer.

So wrapped up in the day and the beauty, and still mentally reeling from the seminar, I had made a fatal error. I had not re-applied sunscreen all day, and by the time we set up camp, I was starting to burn up, not so much with sunburn but with a much worse case of sunstroke as a fever set in.

We camped on the banks of the Snowy River in a spot untouched by human hand. I tried frantically to get myself organised and help with the evening food.

Hamish thought I was just cold again and wasn't at all sympathetic as bush doctors tend to be made of harder stuff. I tried not to moan too much and get on with it, but deep inside I knew I was rough. That night was awful. As I fitted and fevered throughout the night, bad turned to worse as diarrhoea hit. By the morning I was in a bad way.

Now, this was when reality kicked in. We were two days trek into nowhere, no communication and no way out without walking. Hamish was the 'ever-caring' bush doctor, telling me to harden up and get on with it, and ultimately he was right. I had to.

That day we trekked I do not know how many miles along the Snowy River back to Thredbo. It was one of the worst days of my adventures, not quite the worst as that is yet to come, but it is right up there. To top it off, within a mile of leaving camp, I slipped down an embankment and sprained my ankle. Crap. So I moped along behind Hamish for the whole day, just grimacing and trying to get to the next landmark. Little did I know but this test of endurance and perseverance would pay massive dividends in future adventures, particularly serving me well on the Marathon des Sables. But of course I could not see this at the time.

This is where I started to learn to just take the next small step in the journey. I would pick out a landmark and just try to get to that. It was a clumsy strategy but one I would hone in the depths of the Sahara.

We did get back, and I was never happier to see Thredbo and the jeep. For a moment, I swore not to do any deep trekking again. But deep down inside, I was contemplating the next great adventure on my list. This had been such a wonderful trip, with unsurpassable beauty that was ruined by slight negligence in not using suns block and not treating the water properly. It was a lesson in due diligence and careful preparation; a lesson I needed to learn the hard way to prepare me for future adventures.

The grand vision of the Global Grand Slam was now firmly in my mind, and one adventure was ticked off the list. I had started. The question now was "Which one next?" This is the key to a great vision, the ability to break it down into mini visions or sub goals, and ultimately, to break it down to what you can do today. For me it had been to first rebuild my fitness from the ground up to prepare me for the feats of endurance I intended to achieve, starting off with KosciuszKo.

The next year involved a whirlwind of house moving three times and getting married. Although I kept my fitness up, it wasn't until my honeymoon that I got a chance for another adventure. Thankfully, my ex-wife was also an adventurer albeit on a smaller scale. We trekked the full Inca Trail that year, which was just incredible, with no real sagas. I actually held up well in the altitude at 4,000 m—the perfect test for my future high-altitude expeditions. Now, although this wasn't on the adventure vision, I want to point out a second vision I have which is to experience the greatest 100 things on earth, and for me the Inca trail is certainly one of them.

Do not think it is all about one vision. I have multiple.

One financial, one for business, one for health (which dovetails into my adventure one), one for my relationships and also my own personal evolution.

When you create your own visions, go wide and encompass all of life. And get ready to step into it as the adventure continues.

So, what did I decide to do next? … The Marathon des Sables, which would prove to be a battle of the mind and spirit more than I ever thought possible.

Time to work on your vision!

TRUE Thinking on

CREATING YOUR VISION

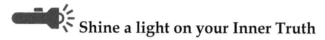 **Shine a light on your Inner Truth**

- If you have clearly identified some bad or negative habits that you want to change, and are committed to change, then you need to focus on them; just one at a time. Define what it is you want to change and do not try to eliminate it; try to **replace it.**

  For example, you could replace: bad food with good food, TV with meditation; surfing the web with surfing real waves ... whatever it is for you. But replace, not eliminate, otherwise it leaves a void. When you think of the replacement, really think through how it makes you feel.

- Focus and monitor your change over 30 days, and set a reward for yourself if you successfully complete it. If you're not successful, don't worry. Just dust yourself down and start again.

  I now speak to those for whom confidence is not a problem. Is your confidence and bravado true? Do you believe in yourself 100%? Are you congruent in that your life is a reflection of your deep passions? Are you moving steady towards your dreams? Or is it hot air? ... Have a good honest think about this. If you're not moving forwards in alignment to your dreams, I challenge you to step up and *make it real.*

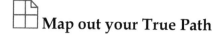

Map out your True Path

Let's look at your dreams, passions or aspirations.

- List 5 examples of who you would like to BE in 1, 3 and 5 years' time

- List 5 things you would like to DO in 1, 3 and 5 years' time

- List 5 things you would like to HAVE in 1, 3 and 5 years' time

- From this create a compelling vision for your life. Make it exciting, make it adventurous. This is your life; create it magnificently.

- Ultimately, it is important to be balanced in your development, so over time try to create compelling visions for all areas. (Health, money, relationships, community, spirituality, career, self-esteem).

- Keep building on this list; it is not static. By the time you reach the final chapter, it will be time to start the process again and refine the wonder even further.

Let your True Guide lead the way

Your beliefs and values can be clearly seen by where you spend your time. Over the next week, be conscious of where your time goes. Look for themes. For example, if you never leave the house without make up on or hair styled, no matter how late you are, then appearance and self-approval are very high values. This is a telling sign of your true beliefs.

- Look carefully for negative traits, like excesses in TV, email or web surfing. The saddest thing I see the most is people who are clear on what they should be doing but just are not doing it. Carefully dissect your time and commit to spending it wisely for it is all we have and it is our most precious asset.

 Identify your inner True North

Create a vision board: In order to really stamp your vision on your subconscious, I recommend creating a vision board. It is what it sounds like: a board with pictures or quotes of your vision pasted on it, designed to motivate and inspire. Our subconscious mind works a lot in pictures, so this can be a huge reinforcement tool. There are plenty of resources around this online, even apps.

Create a positive state of mind: A great way to reinforce new habits is by using a conditioning method called 'Anchoring', which enables you to call up at will a chosen positive state of mind when needed.

A number of motivational speakers, including Tony Robbins, use the anchoring **Power Move**. You need to get yourself into a great state of mind by remembering some time or event when you felt fabulous. As you remember the great feeling you had at the time, anchor that state with a certain move, like pumping your arm or fist, or it could be as simple as touching your elbow.

When you are in deep meditation, you can anchor the state with a touch of fingers. That's why you see meditators sitting in one place with fingers touching; it is anchoring the relaxed state. The trick is to choose a movement that you do not normally do. Then when you do that movement, it will trigger within you that positive state of mind that has now been associated with it. Again, plenty of resources online here.

Chapter 4

Marathon des Sables

PLANNING, PREPARATION AND TAKING ACTION

Life is either a daring adventure or nothing.
~ Helen Keller

"The sandstorm engulfed me fully. I could not see a foot in front of my face. The heat was unbearable and suffocating, on top of trying to breathe through a buff. I was totally covered from head to toe and my layering strategy was paying off. Although the sandstorm wasn't ripping my skin off (like with some other competitors), I was overheating and fighting for breath whilst still trying to keep moving.

The rules say to stop where you are when you are in a sandstorm. I kept moving as to stop now would be the end. So I ran blindly and ruthlessly into the dark, driven by frustration and anger."

This is now the most important chapter of this book and your life, without which all the other chapters become obsolete. So I would encourage you to sit up, breathe deeply and get ready for the adventure.

I am now presuming you have been diligently doing the exercises rather than passively reading this as a typical biography (I know some will come back later to do them and that's okay too). You are now ready to start to make your vision happen. If you have not been doing the exercises, now is the time to decide something. Do you really want to make some change in your life? Do you want to participate fully in life?

Are you ready to step into your own adventure? Or are you going to just passively watch as life goes by? Either way is fine. That is the beauty of this life—we have choice. I just urge you to make that choice a conscious one. If you are ready, then strap in as it is time to take action, real action today, to take that one step closer to your dream.

By now you have some clarity on your **passion**, your **beliefs** and your **vision** of what you will become. So now what? Well, it's time to **take action by setting definable goals** and moving towards the new you, the new adventure. We'll step into it one little step at a time.

I love this chapter and this concept; to me it is the moment where dreams and visions become reality. This is where the rubber hits the road, and you are moving and feeling your way towards your dreams. Life is the journey, not the destination. We will explore this truth more fully in a later chapter. For now, just understand that it is not about the final moment of glory, the moment you summit the mountain, the crossing of the finish line, as that moment lasts mere seconds. It is in the gradual realisation of the goal, and the self-belief and character changes that go with it, where the magic is. Don't get me wrong; the moment of glory is wonderful and the crescendo is always worthwhile. But what you become in the process is what lives with you forever.

For me, the next adventure would be a defining one, one which would give me the belief in myself that I could try anything, be anything and do anything. At the point in my life when I first committed to this, I was far from ready and clueless as to what I would really become as a consequence. The next goal for me on this great adventure was still a million miles away—the legendary Marathon des Sables (MDS), a race of myth and legend, and one where true heroes are shaped.

I can think of no better story on earth to convey the message of setting a big goal and taking one step at a time towards it than this.

So what is the MDS? French for 'Marathon of the Sands', it is essentially six marathons back to back over seven days across the Sahara Desert, carrying everything you need to survive — all provisions, all food. You just get provided with water each day and you choose when you take it, which in itself will prove strategic and critical. Carry too much and you won't make it due to too much weight. Too little and you dehydrate and die. Choose wisely!

Technically, the distances vary with lower distances (half-marathons) on the first and last day. But this is to enable the ultimate in endurance on Day 4. In order for the organisers to claim the coveted title of 'The Toughest Footrace on Earth", on

Day 4 you run a double marathon! 52 miles non-stop across the worst the Sahara can throw at you.

Crazy? Yes. Challenging? Yes. Scary? YES! Amazingly, each year there is a wait list as it gains in popularity as the toughest footrace on earth, the ultimate test of endurance and mental strength.

The MDS has been an enigma for me since my teens. I remember seeing a television program about in my late teens, some Saturday breakfast show demonstrating crazy things people do. I remember thinking that those people must be super-human because normal people could not do that; I could not do that. Then through my early twenties, I came across it more frequently as more TV programs, aided by SKY sports, showed the event as the phenomenon grew and also by hearing that a friend of a friend had completed it.

So, given your passion, beliefs and vision, let's **choose one core goal** that you want to set in your life and ensure it is aligned to your purpose and vision. (We will work on beliefs later, so do not worry about that yet.) Make your goal a stretch, something that makes you feel slightly nervous, something that you're not quite sure you can do. Or if you are feeling particularly adventurous, something you have no clue on how to achieve but want to do it anyway.

My goal was the MDS and to finish, no matter what. And it remained a goal of mine for years, with no real progress towards it until my mid-twenties when I had a wake-up call as to what is possible. This goal would change subtly before the event, but you will see the power of specific and aligned goals later.

But first, let me ask you something. Do you think you could do the MDS? I am not asking if you want to do it because it is crazy and not many people would, but I am asking whether you *could*. If not, why not? I challenge you that anybody could if they truly wanted to. If you are healthy and have two legs, you could.

Now, I realise this must be really testing and stretching your thinking on what is possible, but let me show you how my own paradigm was changed from that type of thinking.

One day I witnessed a profound speaker who had actually done the MDS. Remember, the MDS had been on my list of goals for some years, gathering dust. But after this special day, it was on my 'Things To Do Before I Die' list much more firmly as I had no more excuses. I was working for Mars Inc. at the time, the global chocolate giant, and one year at our yearly conference there was a guy, Chris Moon, who was there doing a motivational speaking slot on the power of the mind and that you can achieve anything you truly set your mind to. He was basing his tale around his life story and his completion of the MDS. The speech in itself was excellent, but the best was saved for a profound moment part way through the speech.

We had already been brought into the motivational element where anyone who can do the MDS is a hero and were all quite pumped. I remember sitting there, thinking *Okay, here is a guy who has done the MDS and he looks quite normal. So I suppose there's no real reason why I couldn't give it a go.* Then in an instant he shattered my paradigm and blasted away any excuses that might have remained. He removed his trousers and showed that he only had one leg! He had completed the MDS with a prosthetic right leg.

He told us of the incredible story of losing his lower right leg and right arm to a landmine and being told he would never walk again. He then not only proved everyone wrong about not walking, but he set himself the extreme goal of completing the MDS, and within a few years he had completed it. He is my true hero. It was only recently, interestingly, that I remembered the fact that Chris had only one arm. It was the sight of his prosthetic leg that had been my big motivator.

That was the day I woke up and decided I am blessed with two arms, two legs, two eyes, two ears and good health, and I can do anything I truly want and set my mind to. (There's that mind and thoughts thing again.) *Given what this amazing man has achieved, what am I really capable of?* What are you really capable of?

Now, if you are still sitting there and have not shaken those excuses yet, then I suggest you go find out what kind of people have already done what you want to do. I think you will find many, many people much, much more disadvantaged than you who have achieved what you want and more. And if you are still convinced you are in the minority, then go for it anyway and be a hero. Be a living example of what is possible, and inspire those around you to greatness.

If you are still a little uncertain or in disbelief after this, then track down people who have done just what you want to do and ask them how they did it. You will find many normal people, just like you, who had a passion and a vision, and step by step they went out there and made it happen.

So, on returning from the Inca Trail in 2005, I signed up for the 2006 MDS, put down my large non-refundable deposit (Yes, you actually pay big money to do this crazy stuff.) and the training began—I had a year. In hindsight, this was stupid and way too little time to prepare for this. Nevertheless, in my over-achieving way at the time it seemed clear and realistic. In contrast, most recently while training for Ironman and gave myself three years, and that is with a relatively good base of fitness. But I needed to learn to swim and have not been on a bike since I was a kid. So I had a little work to do. I now give myself the time I need, though; I have matured a little since my over-zealous youth!

With your own goal, think how long it could realistically take you to reach it if all went according to plan and things fitted in place perfectly. Now add a little extra time, as things rarely go perfectly and to give yourself a little flex. The real time typically lies somewhere between these two extremes: 1) where you know the time to be impossible and it stresses you out just thinking about it; and 2) where it feels easy and you do not feel anxious or motivated at all to get on with it.

Decide on your time frame, set a date and commit now! And do not panic as realism kicks in. This date can be moved, but only moved through a reality check rather than by procrastination. However, the mere act of committing, I can assure you, will set in motion the magic to make the dream a reality.

I had a year to prepare for the MDS. I needed to start somewhere, so I went for my first run. This turned out to be somewhat pathetic. I had been out of peak shape for a while, doing some walking and trekking but very little running. On running just over a mile, I developed asthma and had to stop and walk home. A bad start.

I felt like quitting there and then, as is so often the case. We build a vision in our mind and get to the point of committing and taking action, only to be disappointed in ourselves on the first few outings; hence, we quit.

Think 'New Year resolutions and gym' here. After a quiet word with myself, I decided to learn from past mistakes and plan a realistic training schedule.

I knew my end point (152 miles in seven days), my start point (1 mile) and my time to prepare (52 weeks). After whipping up a quick Excel spreadsheet and a straight line graph in between the two points, I could see what I needed to do each week. For example, in Week 2 I need to run 3 miles, 1 mile/day for three days if necessary. Suddenly things became real and achievable. To this day, I keep my goal tracking as simple as this, although Ironman has complicated this somewhat.

So, where are you now, compared to where you want to be? Be clear and detailed. If it is financial, then measure it. If it is physical, get out and test yourself. Whatever your goal, you need to set a baseline of where you are today. You then map out to where you want to be in detail, and voila you have your gap.

Now, after some time of taking actions, test the timing you previously put in here to see if it still feels realistic and change if necessary.

The key to this whole process is to set manageable steps and increments all the way to your goal so that you know where you need to be each day, week and month. This will keep you focused and on track.

Will you stick to this rigorously? Probably not, but the more you do, the better. This plan is for you to check in against. This is where, if you go off course, you know what you need to do to get back on plan. If your progress is a lot slower or faster than originally planned, you can move your timing accordingly. Either way, you have your steps, and you just need to take the first one. The key to everything is doing something now! And again tomorrow, and next week, and next month…

Now JFDI

I learnt this rather rude phrase in the board room from an old CEO at a company who had it on his strategy slides. He would deliver the strategy or plan, and then at the bottom it would say JFDI, which translated to Just Friggin' Do it. Nothing could sum up the final action more eloquently than JFDI. So, I applied JFDI to the MDS.

Three months out from the event, I was running 25 miles at a time with a pack on my back, and in the last few months I was putting my sessions back to back, culminating in four straights days, a total of 100 miles. It was in these hours upon hours of commitment and dedication that I forged my new character — not during the race itself. To set a goal and be disciplined enough with yourself to stick to it has its own magic.

Your esteem builds as you learn to keep promises to yourself.

I had also changed my whole diet in the process to an alkaline-based one to negate the build-up of lactic acid. This in itself was critical to my success and continues to fuel me to this day. If you want to know more on this and my whole strategy, the best resource is a man I am honoured to call my coach, Stu Mittleman, and his book *Slow Burn* is an absolute must for anyone considering marathons or any form of endurance, or indeed a healthy life. Another great resource is Phil Maffetone, who has also worked alongside Stu, and their combined works are my endurance bible.

Those 100 miles were enough for me. I had intended to run 152 miles, but I felt like I had done enough. I knew I had the distance in my legs. Now, could I handle what the Sahara had to throw at me?

One final thing before we get to the adventure itself. Let's talk *sacrifice* for a moment. Can you have it all?

… No. In order for you to realise some of your greatest goals in life, you have to sacrifice something; it's a trade. You need to replace bad habits with good habits. The countless hours I put into training prior to the event had to come from somewhere. And the excuses about "I don't have time" don't wash either as we all have exactly the same amount. So get over that one, please.

At this time in my life, I was working hard, putting in very long work weeks and was recently married. So, time had to go from somewhere. For me it was letting go of a combination of social life and TV. I stopped watching TV in the evenings and channelled that time towards training. I also cut back hugely on my social life and did not even drink alcohol for the four months prior to the event. Was it worth it? Absolutely. 100%.

Do I miss now those TV programs I skipped? Nope, cannot even remember what they were, and they would not have added any meaningful value to my life anyway. What about social events and those nights out I missed? Again, I would not remember the occasional times down the pub with friends now. I still attended important events like marriages and birthdays, but that was it. What I have in return for these sacrifices is a memory that is unforgettable and will stay with me to the day I die, a memory that has shaped my life.

What I have to say now may sound time- or money- centric, but if you need to save, what will you give up? Smoking? Drinking? Bad fast food habits? Sugar? Coffee? Work it out. A coffee a day at £2 each is over £700 per year. If time is your concern, what is not adding value to your life? Can you cut back on TV? Sleep? (Careful with this one.) Socialising? Gossiping? Whatever it is, decide on your trade and commit. Your vision should be powerful enough to motivate you to do this. If it's not, then you're not thinking big enough. Cut back on work if you are a workaholic. I spend a lot of time with leaders on productivity and can save hours per week by just getting focused and efficient.

The most I have saved is three days per week! The trick then is to channel this saved time into the areas of life you want to make a difference in, like your own great adventure, whatever that may be.

A couple of months before the event, I went to an MDS training day in London that provides top tips from previous competitors. And it was here where I met up with Kate Spicer, a journalist who inspired me to join the Mencap MDS team. This would prove to be the best thing I ever did, and for that I thank you, Kate. A key lesson I was to learn from this decision is that **big goals sometimes need to be part of something even bigger than you.** I was to discover this fully in the heart of the desert, along with some other messages that motivated me along the way … more on that later.

The Mencap team met shortly after for a run on the South Downs, and I realised the team were all super-fit and experienced in various degrees of endurance. Not a great motivational meet for me. The line-up included: CEO of Mencap, Dame Jo Williams, who was an experienced fell runner as was her husband Rob; Brian Jokat, the Canadian pro ice hockey player and Ironman (A big inspiration for my own Ironman exploits); Tim Docker, another fell runner; Bernie, a British running champion; and ex-army guys, Rupert and Alan. We were to be joined later by Emma Sayle, Rachel and of course Kate.

Now, given this impressive line-up, this was not the greatest session for confidence building, and in hindsight it could have crippled me mentally as I was by far the least experienced and, as it turned out on the run itself, the least fit by a long way. I cannot say I did not have moments of fear at this point about my future goals, but thankfully they were still clear and I wasn't going to get sucked in competitively. I was there to finish, not set any records in the process. (So, yes, you guessed it. I finished last!)

Caution on Judgment

Judge yourself on yourself, have your own goals, your own vision, no one else's. Do not get caught in the trap of comparisons, comparing yourself to someone fitter, better, sexier; it is a fool's trap. Just compare yourself with yourself, be the best you can be. There will always be someone better, but that doesn't matter. All that matters is that you are being true to yourself and being the best you can be — no more, no less. I learnt that from my Nan, who always said to me from an early age, "Do your best and leave the rest," and that has stuck with me. Thanks Nan!

I also had a good mentor figure at the time who helped to focus my attention — Dave O'Brien. I met Dave at a talk he gave at an event in Bristol, regaling his tales of the MDS and other endurance events, which was again totally inspiring! Afterwards, when I had the pleasure and honour to meet him personally, we started to discuss the MDS and my imminent departure. During our conversation, he asked me what my goal was, which I was a bit perplexed by so I responded, "Just finish, no matter what."

To this he responded, "If that's what you focus on, that's what you will get." (There's that thought thing again!) "Don't you see?" he continued. "That's what most people in this race think. They see the pain, the heartache, the unbelievable human endurance, and they focus on that. A lot finish, but most in a terrible state, feet bloodied, mentally ruined, unable to walk, and they come home a shell of their previous self. You must ask yourself if there is a better way." … and of course there was.

So, my mantra changed immediately to:

Finish in style with energy to spare and a smile on my face, having enjoyed the journey.

And suddenly my paradigm shifted again. Now remember one very important thing, as quoted by a favourite author and speaker of mine, Mike Dooley: "Thoughts become things." If I had walked into that race with the mentality that it was going to be the toughest thing I ever did, where my feet would be shredded and I would have to drag myself over the line before I collapsed in a heap, then in all likelihood that is exactly what I would have experienced, and I probably would not have completed it at all. As you will see in the following chapters, that did not become my reality because of this shift in my mindset. In the MDS, as in other future mountains, I saw people give up mentally way before they gave up physically. The mind is truly powerful.

The time of the MDS was approaching; it was getting real. Telling people about the challenge became fun in itself, and I cannot describe it better than a fellow comrade in the MDS, Clive Gott (dec.), did in his book:

"When the flag drops, the bullshit stops!"

Person: *"So where are you going on holiday this year?"*

Me: *"I'm going with these idiots here. We have been raising money for two years now, and we are going to walk or run about 150 miles in the Sahara Desert carrying everything we need to survive on our backs. We will endure temperatures in excess of 100 degrees and sandstorms that literally rip your skin off. Our feet will swell, our skin will burn, and we will cry like babies on a daily basis. We will come home completely ****** up both physically and mentally and will not want to face a day at work because of the huge anti-climax we will go through… What about you, going anywhere nice?"*

The training is just a part of it. The kit and logistics are equally critical, as is foot care. I spent months getting my food just right, packing just the right amounts of calories, as the alkaline diet meant I was a vegetarian bordering vegan at the time. Choosing the right footwear, getting gaiters specially made so the sand would not get in my trainers ... So much to think about. I had learnt from my poor planning on previous adventures, and I wasn't leaving anything to chance this time—although, on

Kilimanjaro this would come back to bite me. It is amazing how little you can live on when you are forced to. I was carrying a little pack no bigger than a Tesco carrier bag on my back with everything I would need to survive for a week in the desert, including all food. Everything was weighed, thought through and some things ruthlessly discarded: weight versus pure pleasure. My luxury was an iPod and a solar charger.

What a battle between what we think we want to take and what we need to take. And even after such ruthlessness, we still found after Days 1 and 2 people binning yet more stuff in the battle to keep weight down to a minimum. It makes you really think about life and our material world. What we really need when all is said and done versus what we could actually do without.

So, after months of preparation, it was time; I was ready. Then the week before, disaster struck.

My then partner's father, who had been suffering from cancer for several months, died quite suddenly, just days before the MDS. This threw our lives into turmoil as I was supporting my partner and the family fully, driving all over the UK to get her to her father's side and to the rest of her family to mourn. In the days to come, I had to make one of the toughest decisions of my life. Do I stay with my partner to support her through this tough time or go do the MDS? There was no right answer. One moment I had quit, and the next I was back in, swinging back and forth, agonising over the consequences of each decision. After all the preparation I had put in, all the sacrifice, all the money, all the time, I was finally prepared, and if I backed out now, I would have to do it all again. But how selfish is that? How could I leave when she needed me the most?

This was also shortly after my own father's death, which had been a catalyst that spearheaded my new adventures in life. My father was a great man and one who held a lot of dreams, all of which he was going to accomplish when he retired. He talked about them a lot. He lived his life for 'someday', and 'someday' never came. Just months after his so-called retirement, he died. And although the death was of course sad beyond words, what was sadder still was the loss of the dreams that died with him. I vowed at that point that I would live my life today and refuse to die without my dreams fulfilled.

The death of my partner's father brought all the memories of my own father flooding back to me. This made the decision even tougher as, following his death, I had sworn to seize the day, but now I was hesitating, not without good reason. Thankfully, my decision was made easy for me by my partner who encouraged me to go and supported me 100%.

My euphoria of getting to the MDS was somewhat muted with guilt. I am just thankful for the Mencap team who were just a wonderful bunch and a great support.

We flew to Ouarzazate, Morocco, on 6th April, 2006. We stayed for one night in the wonderful Berbere Palace Hotel, and after eating enough for a week and drinking water to super-hydrate until it was coming out of my ears, it was time to begin the real adventure. And so it began with a very long bus journey of 220 km through Morocco to the deepest part of the desert, Ait Saadane. We were finally making our way to the race's start and, given my super-hydration strategy, I had to make full use of my empty water bottle on the way, as they would not stop the bus.

The buses taking all the competitors just stopped at what seemed like the end of the road in the middle of the Sahara desert. Waiting there was a number of army trucks with the canvas backs taken off. We all scrambled into the back of the trucks and sat in the open desert air. They then careered their way through the desert dunes and took us even deeper into the unknown. Suddenly, on the horizon was our home for the next seven days, what the French call the 'bivouac' – black tarpaulin canvas sheets, raised in Bedouin style with a carpet on the sandy desert floor.

So we settled into our new home. This was the first day prior to the race and was quite busy as there were a lot of final logistics to sort out. Firstly, you had to be signed off medically. This involved getting fully checked by the doctors, plus you had to provide further proof from your home doctor in a signed contract (with full ECG) to say you are medically fit enough to attempt this madness. And then you sign your life away, literally. They also weigh your backpacks. Mine was 18 kg, still a bit on the heavy side for this, but I knew I had fuelled up well for the first few days with extra food to keep my energy up, and my pack weight would drop considerably over the first few days. Little did I know that I would need every ounce of help I could get.

We also were given a water ration card, which was to be all we would be given from there on in, race numbers (Mine was 570) and a flare. If you give up in the middle of the desert with nobody around, you pull your flare and they come and get you. They also checked our compulsory kit which included an antivenom pump in case of snake bites! Nice! And finally, of course, our route books showing the maps and distances for each day. This was essentially a start line, lots of wiggly lines for the sand dunes and a finish point.

As if the desert was testing us, within an hour of arriving at the camp the first sandstorm blew in and we were given a taste of what was to come as sandstorms are a frequent unwelcome visitor every day in the Sahara. I cannot describe the intensity of the storms properly: they were so vicious that exposed flesh would be cut into by the sand, leaving raw, open wounds. Thankfully, my theory of wearing long desert trousers and long sleeves to avoid sunburn was already paying off, and one that would pay massive dividends in the days to come. And so it was time to begin this new adventure, one step at a time…

Time for some planning and goal-setting!

TRUE Thinking on

GOAL SETTING AND PLANNING

 Shine a light on your Inner Truth

- When in the past did you set your mind to do something or made a New Year's resolution and did not follow through? Why not? What stopped you?

- Now, look at your present goal. Do you really believe you can achieve your goal? If not, why not? What are your excuses now? Go deep. If there are excuses or fears, really feel them. Try to understand them and move through them. For any obstacle or excuse, set clear actions of how to overcome them in advance so there are no surprises later on.

- Also, at this point think through if you have really set the bar high enough. Feel free to set it higher but don't go nuts, yet. Just push the boundary a little bit and really start living the adventure fully

Map out your True Path

- Choose a challenging goal that you really want to achieve. Write down the benefits of achieving the goal and why it is so important to you: Why is it a must? Why will you make it so?

- What are you prepared to personally invest or sacrifice to realise that goal? See the long-term pleasure versus the long-term pain and see how this serves you. Really think this through and write down what you're prepared to give up. Commit now.

- What time scale do you choose? Set a deadline for its achievement. Be creative in your time scales and your planning. Make it fun and realistic, and have many points for celebration along the way.

Let your True Guide lead the way

Where are you now in your journey? (Job, financial situation, relationships status, education etc.) Where do you need to be to step into your own great adventure? Who do you need to become? By this I mean which aspects of yourself do you need to improve on or skills do you need to obtain to ensure you reach your final goal? How do you need to behave? Ultimately, what do you need to believe?

- What is your current belief on sacrifice? Do you think it's negative? If you do, how can you now reframe this to see how this actually serves you in the long term?

- Now, do you really believe you can achieve your goal? If not, why not? You can achieve anything. Seek people less fortunate than yourself who have achieved what you want to achieve. Maybe search up on the internet, for example, seeing disabled people do a marathon. Now ask the question again, "Do you really believe it?" If you still don't, then find someone who does believe in you, like a coach or a mentor or even your mum. What else can you do to ensure you follow through this time?

Identify your Inner Truth North

- Act as if you already have it. Visualise, dress up, and just act as if you were already the person who had achieved the goal. This helps the subconscious think it has already happened and increases manifestation. Have fun be the person. Fake it until you make it. Your feelings cannot lie. So, if you can feel it now, it is real if you like it or not.

Time to think about sacrifice again—not in a negative way but as something extremely liberating. What do you instinctively know is not beneficial to you and could be hindering your success? Now look to replace these bad habits or wasted moments with precious moments and good habits that will serve you, allowing your new adventure to enter into your life. Let your subconscious mind guide you.

Chapter 5

Marathon des Sables

ONE STEP AT A TIME

*A journey of a thousand miles
begins with a single step.*
~ Lao-tzu

"I was hanging by my fingers, hundreds of feet from the ground in the midst of the Alps, and what do I do? The one very stupid thing that every film, book and adventure TV show tells you not to do when at a great height: look down. I stared a hundred feet down to jagged rocks and felt what it was like when people joke about their sphincter muscle twitching. That was it. I was here on some stupid mountain, sprawled vertically across a flat rock face I really shouldn't be on, hanging by my fingertips, and I am going to fall and die. And just to make matters worse, I am probably going to shit myself on the way down and die humiliated.

Now my legs were turning to jelly and my left leg started to shake uncontrollably. All I knew was that every ounce of my body was telling me it absolutely wasn't okay to fall, but if I do fall, I will die.

Remember the two fears we are born with – fear of falling and fear of loud noises? Well, I was about to face both; firstly, the fall, and then the loud bang when I hit the floor. And in my head they were both very, very real possibilities."

On life's great adventure, there comes a time when it all becomes real; when the proverbial rubber hits the road. You suddenly find yourself not merely dreaming, visioning, goal-setting, planning and preparing, but actually doing. You find yourself right in the middle of your own adventure. This could be finally standing at the start line of a race, or having your first customer, or lying next to your potential soul mate. This can be exhilarating, exciting, scary or even sometimes terrifying. But once you are in it, this is the moment that counts. This is where you either realise your full potential or step back down to mediocrity.

So, what is it that keeps people on the journey? What keeps the successful people out there living their dreams and staying on their own path? Determination? Motivation? Inspiration? Perspiration? Pure doggedness? Or maybe a little bit of all of the above.

The greatest lesson I have learnt, and the one the desert taught me first-hand, is to just take one more step, no matter how small. In order to do this, you need the ability to be able to perceive the bigger picture. But you also need to be able to break it down into much more manageable, smaller steps, and then have the focus to do just one of them, the next one.

Here comes the power of the mind and the Law of Attraction again. It is within the midst of this process, when you are truly in your adventure, that you need to control your thoughts the most. This is where people bail out; this is where all the uncertainties pop up. This is where any fear of failure surfaces and stares you in the eye. Your mind is either your most powerful ally or your most fearsome enemy. In the desert I faced most of my fears and my mind in its full power and in its most destructive form.

So let's take a journey through the Sahara Desert, through the toughest footrace on earth, on the most difficult year it was ever run. The toughest footrace on earth just got tougher.

Day 1: The toughest footrace begins

We all woke up early, a mixture of nerves, excitement and tiredness, after not really being able to sleep properly on the desert floor that was covered by nothing but a sheet of tarpaulin. The Mencap team was split between two tarpaulin tents, but each morning we all merged as if one. The harsh reality of the desert was becoming clear with the near freezing nights being such a contrast to the searing daytime heat. This morning, like every morning to follow, the bivouac was whisked away before you were barely up and out of it, and sometimes when you were still in it. This was because the organisers needed to get them to the new campsite and set them back up again. Not that they would have any issue with time to set up with me; they could have built a new town by the time I had arrived.

I had hours of preparation each morning, which amazingly were always fully needed. The ritual included taping my feet fully in an attempt at prevention rather than cure, full application of factor 50 sunscreen, pack, repack and pack again. Making sure anything I needed to be at hand was readily available was like some MENSA mind game. But after hours of preparation and plenty of nerves, Number 570 was ready to go.

8 am. We all stood at the start line. The buzz was infectious, the energy a huge rolling wave. Helicopters flew over filming the scene for those people back at home having breakfast on a

Saturday morning whilst watching those crazy people on TV, like I was doing some fifteen years before. At last I was one of those crazy people. The TV buzz was heightened by the presence of Jack Osbourne and his entourage who were in the next tent to us filming a part of his endurance series. The start was more like a pop concert than a race, but that was soon to change.

The butterflies in my stomach were the size of albatrosses. I was excited but terrified; I was confident but fearful. The intensity of the feat I was about to undertake was overwhelming, and I was about to discover how much success or failure was to do with the mind. I thought I was entering a physical challenge, but in truth I was going beyond MENSA. The next six marathons and seven days were to be the biggest mental challenge and the biggest discovery of my life to date.

The gun went off, people were shouting and cheering, the music was playing, and we all started running in a mad frenzy into the nothingness that is the Sahara.

After an initial ten minutes of running in euphoria and excitement, a lot of people got the reality check and started to slow down and keep their pace in check as we had a long way to go. I think some got carried away in that first day and set the pace way too high in the excitement of it all. This would prove to be a fatal error in the hours to come. Adrenalin can serve you or sink you. If you harness it properly, it can see you through.

If you get carried away in the euphoria of it all, you can blow your tanks before you have barely begun. That is applicable to all areas of life.

The first few hours were crazy and still great fun, running through some Bedouin villages deep in the Sahara. Children lined the tiny dirt tracks, cheering on the crazy foreigners who dared to come into their domain, running in a land where you just do not run. The children had their hands out and were high-fiving all the runners, still excited, on their way through. As I was approaching, I had my hands up ready to do the same when a guy at the side of me said in a broad Aussie twang, "You don't want to do that, mate. They're high-fiving with their left hand." I looked at him quizzically with no clue as to what he was meaning. "Eat with your right hand, wipe your arse with your left, mate," he said, smiling, as he ran on. Now, to this day I do not know how accurate his advice was, but needless to say I did not high-five anyone. And the onset of diarrhoea? The next 48 hours miraculously passed me by without incident.

Although this was a short day at 28 km, the organisers threw in a range of steep hills right in the middle of the course just to test us, which was really tough and totally unexpected. This meant clambering up steep, rocky slopes on our hands and knees at times; as if we did not have enough to battle in the desert. It was like putting a steep, rocky mountain in the middle of the London Marathon on a searing hot summer's day. But then this was the toughest footrace on earth, so what did I expect? The rest of Day 1 for me was a blur, fuelled by adrenalin.

Another sandstorm kicked in towards the end of the race, and this time I did not have the luxury of the tent to protect me. Visibility was down to zero as I battled on through it. And then suddenly I was done. I collapsed in a heap with the desert unleashing its full fury all around me—my first mental test. I felt finished already, the heat, the sandstorm, the intensity of it all. Physically, I was feeling broken, but in reality it was my mind that was breaking first. All the doubts came rushing in like a fire hydrant unleashed. *This is Day 1 and I am feeling like this already. I shouldn't be here? Why am I here?* I sat there stewing in my own negative thoughts for what felt like an eternity. *How much further? And why did I break so quickly? It happened so fast. This must be the wall again.*

And then the storm started to settle and visibility started to clear. Out of nowhere the finish line emerged just in front of me. I had collapsed a mere few hundred yards from the end, unable to see it. Up I bounced and dashed over the line. WOW. What an incredible metaphor. What a lesson. How many of us are wrapped up in our own little sandstorms of negativity, unable to see the finish line just ahead? This gave me plenty to think about. I had done Day 1, though. I had started the race super-hydrated: I had drunk 9 litres of water and not peed once! This was brutal!

The one thing that kept me focused each and every day was thinking of the moment I would cross the finish line and go straight to the communications tent to call my family. Before I did anything, before I drank, ate or stretched, I would just sit there in the queue for up to an hour, waiting to use the satellite phone to have just a few minutes talking to those I loved. This call became a major motivator and driver for me each and every day and got more and more emotional as the race continued.

That first night, I was very pleased to be home in the tent, lying in the sand with only five-and-a-half marathons to go. But something did not feel right. I knew it was tough, but so tough already? Then the stories started to come in. People were already dropping out from heat overload and the soaring humidity.

Fifty dropped out on the first day, which was unheard of. People just do not drop on the first day. We were already part of an unprecedented brutal race. The toughest race of the toughest race on earth just got tougher.

Day 2: Let's start up a mountain

Another marathon in the desert. *What on earth am I doing out here?* To top it all off, once a night-time sandstorm had cleared and we woke up in the morning, we found ourselves staring up a great big hill right in front of us. At the time I called it a mountain.

But since then I have climbed real mountains, so this was a very, very big hill.

To keep the high reputation of being the toughest foot race on earth, the organisers keep pushing the boundaries each year, and this year they were truly exceeding themselves. Today, our worst fears became real as they started the course with a 3 mile run up the 'mountain' pass at 9 am in the full heat of the desert. I, like most people, just kicked back and walked it uphill, as things were already on the edge. But even that hurt.

I was now officially stripped of any material worldliness. All trivial thoughts in my mind were removed, and I was left with pure survival instinct and raw emotion. I would be running one moment and then in tears the next, crying for no reason—joy, happiness, pain, the thought of my wife. It was a totally cleansing experience and a very unnatural experience at the same time. And believe me, I am no crybaby back in the real world. But this day, and every day following this, took me to my limits.

This day is remembered as 'Sandstorm Day' as the sandstorms seemed to last for most of it. It was a weird and dangerous sensation as the wind was drying any sweat you produced and, although the sun was blocked out by the storm, the heat was just as intense. I think this must be the closest you get to sitting in the oven at gas mark 4.

Today I met Roy, a Canadian legend of the MDS who gave me further inspiration during a tough day. Roy had been a professional rugby league player when one fateful day, some years before, he had broken his neck playing rugby. The doctors told him that he would never run again. I was in tears as he told his tale, but I don't think he noticed as the sandstorm was drying them out as quickly as I was crying them and we both had our desert goggles on. We walked/ran together for over an hour, and that guy did not moan once, although we were both having a bad day. And despite the carnage that was to come, he crossed the finish line in the end. To me, he is the true hero of that race.

This is where the thoughts of fear, uncertainty and pure negativity started to clear, as a much bigger voice was taking their place. A voice of gratitude, a voice of courage and a voice of certainty. Hearing Roy's tale made me realise I had nothing to complain about. I have two legs and can walk, so just get on with it and take one more step. It brought me back to the initial inspiration by Chris Moon, with his one leg and one arm, who had done this. So time for me to shut up and put up.

I don't even remember getting in that day. I just remember the day being gruelling and hearing the stories that another load of people had dropped out. Now it was getting a bit close to home as two of our tent members had now dropped as well—two very experienced and fit people. The doubts were starting to creep back in.

Day 3: Another marathon, of course

This was the day when the reality of what we were undertaking really kicked in. It started like all the other days: line up, cheer, sing Happy Birthday to whichever poor sod had dragged themselves into the desert on their special day, gun goes off and just keep going. One step at a time, over and over and over.

Another day of carnage, more people dropping out and people on drips everywhere. This is where I discovered a cool new rule of the race: Three drips and you're out! What a crazy rule that is! Surely *one* drip and you're out. But in this mad world I had entered, it appeared medically okay to get people on a drip then send them back into the desert. I actually fancied a couple myself at times, and I know several people who had their quota of two. It almost became a strategic target, like a chocolate bar mid-afternoon. But my thoughts were to save your drip until you really, really need it.

Halfway around, I hit the hardest single point of the whole race. We were faced with another vertical rock face, with the highest dunes I had seen yet meandering their way to the top—just for the fun of it. I saw a helicopter come in and land at the top as I was approaching, but I had no time to wonder about its purpose as I battled with the slope itself. At the time, getting up that steep sandbank was torture, one step up, two steps back. It was frustrating and agonising and just sapped you of the very little reserve of energy you had left whilst getting nowhere. Just like some points in life where you think you're making all the right moves but seem to be going nowhere, even backwards.

So I just stopped and took another look. Maybe there was another way. I was, after all, just following some other French people. How did they know this was the right way, anyway? So I stood back, picked out a slightly different route and decided to throw myself at it. I used all my reserves and just attacked the hill with pure brute force.

When I got to the top, the expenditure of energy just floored me. The adrenalin disappeared and I collapsed, exhausted in a heap, not even taking my pack off. It took me ten minutes to recover from that ordeal. I watched with detachment the frenzy of activity all around me. I soon realised the hill had had the same effect on most others. Organisers were running everywhere, loads of people on drips, several on stretchers. People with bloodied feet cried out in agony as the doctors tried to cut open the blisters and dip their raw feet in iodine. Amongst it all, somebody was being stretchered off into the helicopter … *must be serious*. It was like a war zone. I drank some more water, threw my pack back on and ran off down the slope back into oblivion. As I did so, a flare went off in the near distance, another one down. I was so glad to leave that hill. My senses could not take in such frenzy anymore after acclimatising to the silence of the desert.

The day continued … sand, sand and more sand. Finally, seeing the end in the distance, and knowing I was so close, I really slowed down and took my time. I hit the final checkpoint, jubilant, only to be told if I did not get my arse in gear I would miss the cut-off point and be out of the race! What? I consulted with my map as I did not understand and realised I had made a fatal error. For Day 3 there were *two* pages of maps, and I had only got to the end of the first page! Bugger.

So, I turned the page to see another 8 km to go, which included three mountain ridges and a 5 km plateau. To add fuel to the fire, in came the biggest sandstorm yet.

The sandstorm engulfed me fully. I could not see a foot in front of my face. The heat was unbearable and suffocating, on top of trying to breathe through a buff. I was totally covered from head to toe and my layering strategy was paying off. Although the sandstorm wasn't ripping my skin off (like with some other competitors), I was overheating and fighting for breath whilst still trying to keep moving. The rules say to stop where you are when you are in a sandstorm. But I did not have time and knew that to stop now would be the end. So I ran blindly and ruthlessly into the dark, driven by frustration and anger.

This misjudgement of the route could have broken me mentally, and I know several others made the same error and some did not finish that day. But now I was mad and this anger fuelled me the rest of that day.

Although effective energies, they're not ones which are sustainable or fulfilling.

The sandstorm lasted another hour and did not ease up until I was halfway across the plateau. I did not stop until I could see the camp a mere quarter of a mile away as I ran into an oasis. I checked my watch and did not have long to go — minutes to be precise. But there in front of me, like the ultimate temptation, was a huge, lush, luxury bath in the middle of an oasis! Okay, it was probably a drinking trough for the camels, but to me it looked like a luxury spa.

Oh, the dilemma. Jump in the water and splash about in pure ecstasy but risk missing the cut-off point, or run to the finish and miss this moment of bliss. As I stood there and debated, another guy flew past me and just jumped straight in. I needed no more convincing as I plummeted after him. To this day, that was the best and loveliest bath I have ever had. We just lay there in the water for a few minutes, the sand washing off us, the cool water engulfing us in pure bliss. Then it was shattered with shouts from the organisers about the cut-off, and we dragged ourselves out of Nirvana and careered along the route with newfound energy, dripping wet, to the finish line.

What I discovered later was that well over 100 people had dropped out by now, and we were in a real saga. I also discovered that the helicopter from earlier was taking out two competitors who had slipped into a coma. That night, as we sat in our tent after hearing the news, was a very soul-searching and sobering time.

We really were pushing the edge of human endurance, so much so that two people are close to paying the ultimate price. Is this really worth it? How far do you push it? When is enough enough? And how do you know when you are there?

Thankfully, our tent camaraderie made up for the gloom. Brian Jokat, in particular, got me through that desert. He wore a pair of 'Love It' pink shorts, which kind of summed him up. His constant cursing, shouting and jokes made the gloomiest of moods lighten. Between him and Tim Docker, we were now the only ones left in the race in our tent, the other members of the Mencap team in our tent had now dropped. All the others had dropped. As such, we bonded closer than ever, encouraging each other and also goading each other with humour. I soon became 'Green Man' due to the green drinks and vegetarian food I was eating and 'Tin Man' as I was certainly no Ironman at the time; the start of my future quest for Ironman began here.

Another person I will never forget is Katie. Despite all the chaos, dirt and dust of the desert, she sat there and applied make-up and nail polish. When I questioned the absurdity of it, she sat there quite calmly saying it is what keeps her happy and that was all that mattered. And she was right. We all needed our little luxuries and to just do what makes us happy. Mine was a mini chocolate pudding, which never tasted better.

In the heart of the desert, the simplest of things could become pure bliss. You regain an appreciation of life that we so easily lose in our mad, frenzied, material world. And each of us in that desert was seeking what it was that made us happy. We were all peeling back the onion to see what lay at the very core, and to me it was love ... the pure love of my wife, family and friends that I left behind.

By now four out of the twelve members of the Mencap team had dropped out—the most unlikely four, as they would have been the ones I would have placed my money on. Despite having to face their own demons, their teamwork and camaraderie were incredible. They were out of the race, yet these four guys chose to stay in the tents. They could have gone to the organiser's camp in comfort, but they stayed to give the rest of us moral support. This support was going to be greatly needed in the days to come. During this time, the CEO of Mencap, Dame Jo Williams, stood out as a true leader, and her unwavering support for everybody was inspirational as was her dedication to the cause we were all running for. Jo, I honour you.

Things were getting emotional now, and what really topped that emotion were messages received in the evening. I did not get any messages the first two nights, but now they started streaming in, that night and every night. Friends and supporters back home could follow our progress online and send us wishes of encouragement and love. Each night the organiser would come around the camp shouting your name and you'd go to get the messages. I kept these messages on me at all times. The encouragement I felt from friends, my wife and from the Mencap team was incredible. It often brought a lump to my throat, and I would have to go out to the dunes for another little cry disguised as a toilet stop. Here are just a few messages that got me through the desert. They speak for themselves. Thank you to all who sent me a message. Each was gratefully and emotionally received.

"Much as I'd love to tell you what a sissy you really are, I am in fact proud to see you do this thing. It's a far cry from Coogee when you couldn't keep up with me for 500m. I am in no doubt that you are now slightly nervous and wondering what you've gotten yourself into. I am also wondering what you've gotten yourself into. But you're a superstar and you can do it. When I run a marathon (or an ultra), there is always a point when it starts to hurt. I always find comfort in the following thought: No matter how much it hurts, I know I can take twice as much pain and still finish the damn race. Godspeed — wind in your back — may you run like the wind! P.S. I hate you for raising the bar. I am going to have to come up with something even more challenging, and my body is not getting any younger."

~ Mark Prinsen (The Dutch Lion)

"Hello, I've been following you on the website. It looks amazing! You've reached the end of another day! Your determination is a real inspiration.

Staying determined in such a harsh environment is a battle. Please remember that while most of us stay within our comfort zone most of the time, avoiding the things we find difficult, people with learning disabilities know about battling. Many of them find everyday things difficult, things that we take for granted, but they don't have the luxury of giving these things up. They can't get other people to do everything for them either, nor would they want to. People with a learning difficulty can learn and achieve a lot in a life if they have the right support. Your support this week will help to make this happen. Stay focused and let the battle commence for another day."

~ Kate Tintner MENCAP

And battle it would be...

When the going gets tough, never underestimate the power of someone giving you support and encouragement, someone believing in you. It can make all the difference in the world. Make a pact to yourself today to be that spark of inspiration to the people around you. Give people support. Do not be the doomsayer and the critical one, the breaker of dreams. Be the maker of dreams.

Day 4: Not one marathon but two

Day 4 was the dreaded double: two marathons, back to back over 52 miles. With a field already more than decimated, we all faced this with angst and trepidation. But face it we did. The veterans lined up on the start line. We had battled through three of the toughest days the MDS had ever seen, and we were still standing.

Today was D-Day and for me a defining day in my life.

The day went on and on, and many times I felt like quitting. I was emotionally broken by now, physically as well. You are stripped of everything material and are just thinking of survival. Water, food and the next step is all that matters. In such a situation, what you are left with is who you are. Mostly, I was thinking of my wife and my family. I would be running and the next minute in tears, thinking how I missed them so much. This was an epiphany for me as work no longer mattered, and if I had died there and then it wasn't the office hours, the deals or the work success that mattered. What truly mattered was whether I had really told those around me that I loved them. Had I loved fully, and what was my legacy? So there in the middle of the desert, I discovered life's true purpose: to live fully, to love and be loved, and to leave a legacy.

In the final moments, that is all that truly matters, and that includes loving yourself.

I also learnt one more thing. When life is tough and you are at the end of your tether and feel you can no longer go on, you can always take one more step, and that was all I could focus on. To think of another 30 miles, another marathon, another half-marathon, would have destroyed me, so I just focused on the next step. I would pick out a mound, a bush, a rock, something in the near distance, and make it my goal. I would head for it unwaveringly and once I got there, I would reward myself with a swig of water and do it again. Sometimes when there was nothing to see in the distance, I would just do ten more minutes and reward myself with a bite of a snack, a sweet, anything. And with that routine, one step at a time, I would break the back of the infamous double. One small step, reward, repeat.

That approach got me through most of the double, but as night was approaching and with still 15 miles to go, I finally felt I had had enough and hit another wall. I had been asking myself for hours why on earth I was doing this. *Why push myself to the limits? What am I proving? Why am I here?* My mind had been taking over, and I was starting to lose the mental battle again. I wanted to give up. I just needed to collapse, open my pack and pull a flare. The camels would come along and I would be carried out. So, why carry on? *Why God, why?*

Now, firstly, do understand I am not a deeply religious person, although I think the essence of all religion is good. I am more spiritual in nature and believe truly in something far bigger than ourselves. I call it 'God and the Universe', you can call it whatever you wish. But whatever 'it' is, I was talking to it.

I could see no one either ahead or behind; I was truly alone in the vast expanse of the Sahara. *Having completed nearly four marathons in four days whilst carrying everything I needed to survive, and with over two marathons to go in the 'toughest footrace on earth', I had nothing left. I was broken, physically and emotionally. It was just me and my spirit, or what was left of it, remaining.*

In the midst of the Sahara Desert, I dropped my pack and collapsed onto my knees on the sand — spent. I looked up to the heavens, to the overwhelming beauty of the stars and the universe, and just shouted, "Why the bloody hell am I doing this? Why me? If I am truly meant to do this, then give me a sign because I'm done!" After my ranting subsided, I sat in the silence.

Just the release of shouting my frustrations into the nothingness was therapy enough. I relaxed, let go and took a deep breath. Then the unexpected happened.

I got my answer. It began as an ethereal sound in my head. I can only liken it to journeys in deep meditation or the work with spirit guides I have done in the past. It is something I will never forget. Initially, I was a little scared as I thought I had finally gone mad — and I might well have been according to some. But there I felt the full presence of God / Spirit that night in the desert. I had my first truly enlightened experience ... and there would be more to come in my future adventures.

But I felt immense peace as I heard ...

Deri, you are all you need to be right now. You don't need to prove or do anything more, you never have. You are doing this as you wish to experience great adventure and experience, everything that this world has to offer, and that includes experiencing yourself fully. Know that I am proud of you. You are truly testing yourself to the limits right now and exploring the depths of your soul. Nothing will faze you after this. Imagine, once you have completed this race, you will carry that through the rest of your life and you will never say 'can't' again.

I stayed still as the voice soothed to a stop and the desert stilled. I was left alone in silence. An energy swept over me. I was clear now. This was all about really discovering myself and connecting to my soul. I had peace. I had nothing to prove. Ego was lost.

And then, to add to the magic, I saw a glint in the sand just ahead. I got up and walked towards it; it was a ring. A beautiful, silver Arabic ring. And I smiled. A sign. I felt goosebumps all over my body. To this day, I marvel at the miracle of finding that small ring in the whole of the Sahara Desert at that precise moment, and I wear it around my neck as a wonderful reminder of the magic around us when things in life appear to get tough.

I stayed in that place for a little while, cooked dinner and watched the stars rise in the incredible clear sky of the Sahara.

What had been a self-created hell one hour earlier suddenly became heaven on earth. Moments in life are what we choose them to be; the power of the mind is inconceivable.

We choose our thoughts and create our existence around us. One person's heaven is another person's hell. I choose the former.

The night went on. I ran, shuffled and walked onwards in the darkness, guided by a laser beam that was projected into the sky from the finish line and could be seen for miles around. It was quite surreal, stumbling through the desert with an Ibiza-like laser light to guide me. I never stopped again that night and I got in around 2 am, the second one to arrive in our tent. Brian was ahead of me already, curled up on a carpet, dead to the world. No carpets were on the floor this night, so I went and stole one from the organisers' quarters, as by this point I really did not care. Then, after my double marathon through the Sahara, I slept — deeply.

When you can spend that much time with yourself alone and enjoy the experience whilst retaining some sanity, you are truly close to discovering who you really are. The extreme adventures I do are a kind of ultimate life-school where I learn life's great lessons by doing. No book, seminar or teacher can do it in quite the same way; it is something you have to experience.

We had the next day to rest, which was much needed.

Around midday, the last person came over the line to triumphant applause. I was jubilant, having gotten over the worst part of the race and surviving when a record number of people had dropped out. It made me feel invincible, and I just knew I could do it now; nothing could stop me. After all, I had received divine inspiration.

I also received two of the most moving messages of the trip:

"I think you should now have completed the mythical 72 km stage – what a massive accomplishment! I hope that knowing you are supporting Mencap is helping keep you motivated. And although it's not quite time for you to put your feet up – when you do, you'll certainly have earned yourself a break (and a beer). Imagine how you'd feel if you couldn't see the end of this week – if this extraordinary hard work that you're doing was never going to end? That's the reality for thousands of people caring for loved ones who have a learning disability.

The impact on their lives, and the lives of their families, is enormous. It is vital that carers have access to quality respite care, so that they can go on with their caring role. By supporting Mencap, you are helping us carry on our fight for better support for carers. It really does make the difference. Thank you."

~ Kate Tintner, Mencap

"Superman speaks: I think a hero is an ordinary individual who finds strength to persevere and endure in spite of overwhelming obstacles. (Christopher Reeve)... You know what to do."

~ James Richardson

And then the next morning the worst possible thing happened, as if to test my resolve to the very limit.

Day 5: How much can I really take?

I woke in the middle of the night with just one more marathon and a half-marathon on the final day to go. I had gone to bed feeling jubilant, and now I was feeling sick. My stomach was turning over and I was feeling nauseous. I crept from my sleeping bag and the freezing desert night just encapsulated me. I shivered my way to the nearest dune as I was desperate for the toilet, but I did not get more than twenty paces. I won't go through the next five hours, but needless to say I had diarrhoea badly. In the comfort of your own home, this is not a good thing. In the desert, where hydration is half the game, it is a disaster, and already a big reason why a lot of people had dropped out. This was a game changer.

Two hours before the start of the day, I thought it was all over, and I just lay back on the sand to gather my thoughts. I had been focused for the last five hours on the fact that it was all over for me. I could not possibly go on now. So many people had already dropped due to this. Why now? Why me? Boo hoo. And there it was again, 'thoughts become things'. The only way I was to have any chance of this race was to change my thought, and change it quickly and consciously.

So I gave myself a mental slap and picked myself up. I had to reframe my thinking, and fast. How could I go on? What could I do to finish? If this was a life and death situation and I had to finish, what would I do?

This was the day of Naomi's father's funeral, and I wasn't there with her because I was here. Was I to give it all up so easily? I felt the ring around my neck; there had to be a way.

Suddenly the answer was clear. Go take some tablets that block you up as you only have another 36 hours left. Go beg, borrow and steal as much toilet paper as you can. Take your maximum quota of water with you as the pack had lightened considerably, and just get on with it. And that's exactly what I did. During the first four hours of that day, I went to the toilet a further five times. Run, stop, splash, wipe … Run, stop, splash, wipe ... You get the picture. But each time I double-hydrated. I finished that day, not in great time, but I finished. And that was good enough for me. Now I knew I had cracked this beast, and I had recreated myself in the process. I would never be the same again.

As I came into the camp, jubilant at my finish, I was faced with one of the most surreal sites I have ever witnessed. There under the setting sun was a full orchestra and an opera singer creating some of the most magical music I have ever heard. And there sitting in front of the temporary stage watching were not ladies in dresses and men in tuxedoes, but comrades wrapped in foil blankets, lying on the bare sand, exhausted but triumphant, with a bottle of water or a tin cup in their hands.

Another message was waiting.

"You can do it! It sounds like a cliché but I know you can do this. You are the strongest, most unique and determined person I have met or probably will ever meet. I have every ounce of faith in you. You'll complete this and run through the finish line with a smile on your face and think that everything that you have worked so hard for has paid off. You have just got to keep your eye on the road. Think of what you are doing this for and what a difference it is making to the lives of people with MS. You have a tremendous amount of courage, intellect and spirit, and I know you're gonna go far, coz you've worked for it, and you deserve every merit that comes your way. So chin up, and most importantly GOOD LUCK, with all the love in the world, and a massive hug."

~Laura (my sister)

The Final Day

The final day was upon us, for those who were left. I was still not feeling great physically, but was strong emotionally and mentally. Nothing was stopping me now. The start line was like the first day, full of music, cheering, chanting and TV cameras as the survivors of the 21st MDS careered into the desert for one last time.

I ran all the way, up over the highest dunes in the Sahara Desert, as if we had not endured enough! I do not know where my energy came from that day. It was boundless. I was running up and down the dunes like a madman. I went down one so fast I tripped, did a full forward role with my pack still on, bounced back to my feet and kept on running. It appeared nothing could stop me.

And suddenly, out of the big dunes ahead, I could see the banners. I could hear the cheering, and I could actually see the finish line. I sprinted that last 300 yards as fast as I could, and I cannot describe in words the feeling of that moment, arms in the air, with the crowds cheering as I neared the finish line. That feeling will stay with me for a lifetime. Just then I caught up with Tim Docker, my fellow teammate and tent mate, and we ran in together, which was perfect. I crossed the line, was embraced by the founder and the medal placed over my head.

For that moment alone it was all worth it. **I finished with energy to spare, in great style, with a smile on my face**, just like I had envisioned. In fact it was far, far better than I could ever have imagined.

Years of thinking, visioning, goal setting, over a year in training, all the planning, the preparation, the sacrifice, the sweat, the blood, the tears, all cumulated in that one moment, the moment of completion. Would I do it again? Never. Was it worth it? Absolutely!

This is what the press had to say about it:

"MDS lives up to its reputation as the most difficult race in the world. Director Patrick Bauer looked back at this year's race where 146 people pulled out. Bauer explained that this unusually high level was due to extreme weather conditions (even for the Sahara) from Day 1: temperatures up to 42 degrees, sandstorms and very high hygrometry levels of up to 35%. Nature took over. You realise how small you are compared to the elements. In these conditions what counts is having good mental and physical preparation. To those who did finish, I take my hat off to you."

~ www.darbaroud.com

In addition there were a record number of 62 IVs administered and a severe case of hyperthermia, the first on a MDS.

So what about your own personal MDS?

So take your own goal, your own MDS, and break it down. Break it into manageable steps, and ultimately take something you can do right now in this moment and go do it. Have things you can do today, this week this month, and just keep moving step by step towards your dream. The first steps will be small, maybe even exploratory. Find out more, get the price, get the date, who you can talk to; whatever it is, just do it. And keep doing it. The secret to achieving goals, living your passion and stepping into your vision is not one big massive moment where suddenly, as if by magic, you've done it all. It is a build-up of lots of little steps, one at a time, and then all you need is a little patience to make it all happen. That will be the next lesson.

At those moments in my life when times get tough, things are not going quite right or I feel like quitting, I stop and think about the MDS and what I achieved. I hold my desert ring in my hand and everything suddenly seems minor in comparison. I check my thoughts to ensure they are serving me, and if they are not, I change them and change them fast.

A lot of spiritual teachers have had experiences in the remotest parts on earth, even Jesus spent forty days and forty nights in the desert; I only did seven, though I was running for most of them! I have also heard tales of great teachers learning lessons whilst climbing mountains; from such great heights day-to-day things seem minor in comparison.

So, I set my heart on mountains, on the next great adventure and the rest of the Seven Summits, starting in deepest darkest Africa.

Time to take action!

TRUE Thinking on

TAKING ACTION

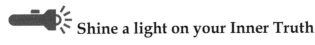 **Shine a light on your Inner Truth**

Write down a vivid description of what it feels like to achieve your goal. Use all your senses. What does it feel like, taste like, smell like? What can you see and what can you touch? Does this excite you? Feel this now, and imagine stepping towards it, one step at a time.

- If this feels great, then do this as often as you can: in the car, on the bus, whilst walking. Get into the habit of seeing your dream before you. Most nights I dream of summiting Everest.

- Now you know how it feels to achieve your goal or dream, set a reward for achieving it, something even more tangible than the dream itself.

- Some people need the twin motivation of positive and negative. So think now about how it would feel not to achieve it. Fast forward 5 – 10 years. How does it feel now if you take no action, you do nothing and you continue to live a life of mediocrity? This is the consequence of your non-action. Now, you choose which one you want.

Map out your True Path

- Think through what are the next small steps you need to do to start to slowly step into your adventure. List them and commit to doing one or more in the next week. Today would be great. Think small to start off with. This can be just making a call, finding out more information, surfing the web, signing up to a marathon…

- Think through your ideal week, yes ideal. Where is your time spent in your ideal week? Now look at where your time is really going. Commit to scheduling some time for your small action steps each week, and figure out when that will be.

Let your True Guide lead the way

- Now it is time to really start to own your thoughts. Keep a very close eye on them. For some people, journaling is a good way to keep track of their thoughts and emotions. Learn from your reflections and keep a watchful eye on patterns, both positive and negative. Your thoughts become things, so own them. You must believe this.

Identify your inner True North

- Do not let your subconscious control you. Keep careful. Watch over any overriding negative thoughts or fears. Challenge them. Are they real? If so, on what basis? It's time to take control of your thoughts, harness them and let them serve you, not hinder you

- Let your subconscious work for you overnight. Before bed, ask yourself, "What are the next main steps I need to make tomorrow? If I had to do just three things tomorrow, what would they be?" Write down whatever comes to mind and put this on your bedside table. Sleep on it. Your subconscious will do the work. When you wake up, check those three things, and if they still feel right, just do them no matter what. First things first, that day and every day.

Chapter 6

Kilimanjaro, in the Death Zone

PATIENCE AND PREPARATION

A mind is like a parachute.
It doesn't work if it is not open.
~ Frank Zappa

"The next day we started the trek into BaseCamp, and I was buzzing. With full pack on, which was quite heavy at 40+kg and dragging a sled of team equipment behind me of equal weight, I felt invincible as we glided down the slope and onto Denali proper. This was what real exploring was all about; this was going to be the biggest adventure yet!

The downhill turned to uphill quite quickly, and that did not change for the next three weeks. Within two hours, I was totally knackered and was calling on every last bit of reserve I had to get me through the first day. This was going to be terrible, and I wanted to go home. Imagine this, you are carrying a full pack on your back, weighing 40kg, and on top of this you are dragging a sledge behind you with another 40kg in it, all up a very big hill! No, up a mountain through snow and ice. And it is cold, very cold. I wasn't fit enough, and I knew it."

The next great adventure

I had prepared incredibly well for the Marathon des Sables, and in hindsight a large part of my success was directly attributable to my intense preparations. Thinking through each detail and ensuring I had the right kit, the right medical, the right fuel, all paid off.

And so you would think that particular life lesson well embedded, right? But such is life in that unexpectedly we get a more profound lesson when we least expect it.

It was on the second of the Seven Summits, Kilimanjaro, where I received two life lessons, both delivered in a very powerful way. Firstly, the 'pole pole' lesson. The porters constantly chant this in Swahili, meaning 'slowly slowly', or to put it another way, patience. Secondly, the importance of planning and preparation, again. I must admit that patience is not one of my strongest virtues. When God was handing all the virtues out, I think I must have been in the toilet or taking a snack break when she was handing out 'patience'. Just ask my wife about me and queues. As such, sometimes life lessons need to be taught gently and sometimes they need to be taught hard. Kilimanjaro would teach me a hard lesson in patience and planning and test me to the absolute limit.

Why is patience such a necessary virtue on life's great adventure? We live in a world of convenience. We expect everything now and yesterday, and this includes our goals. I chuckle at the popularity of *The Secret* and the whole draw of the Law of Attraction. Although the lessons are indeed powerful and profound, a lot of people still expect to wave a magic wand and voila, all their hearts' desires are manifested immediately. When they do not immediately transpire, some dismiss the concept as hocus pocus and move onto the next fad, seeking the one silver bullet—the one which will give them what they seek immediately and with no work. I recognise this as it used to be me. What I have learnt through my adventures in life is that while the vision, belief and goals are key, patience, focus and dedication are needed to ensure our dreams indeed materialise.

Step-by-step action is key, but do realise that there is a gestation period, like any seed you plant. Using a gardening analogy, it is like planting a seed and then going back the next week and not seeing any shoots and throwing it away. Anyone who has gardened knows each seed has a gestation period, and although they sometimes take a while to shoot, with the right nurture, conditions and with a bit of luck, a certain percentage will shoot. Ironically, some of the most beautiful plants and flowers have the longest gestation period of all, some taking months. Think about that.

So, nurturing the seed (your goal), holding the belief consistently and constantly no matter what buffers you along the way, and holding on to the *feelings* of your desire right now, are key to your progress. Having the patience to do this 'pole pole' (slowly, slowly) will keep you sane and on track. I learnt this and much more on what was to be a truly humbling journey of discovery on Africa's highest mountain.

Note that I use the word 'feeling' above. What is it in a goal, vision or desire that we truly seek? The object or the photo we get at the summit? No. I propose now that it is the *feeling* we are seeking. And the next adventures for me would truly teach this, but I don't want to spoil the crescendo here. For now, just start thinking about what feeling it is you are seeking, and start to try to feel it now; imagine it, vision it, feel it.

The adventure begins...

Following the Marathon des Sables (MDS), I had no immediate plans for my next adventure as I was trying hard to recuperate physically, mentally and emotionally. Some two to three weeks after the event, I was suffering Post-MDS-Depression. Depression is quite common after huge endurance feats. After you have pushed yourself to the limit, coming back to normal, everyday life can be relatively depressing, which can cause you to re-evaluate your life in many ways. This is where I think the endurance bug lies, constantly pushing to see what the miracle of the body and mind can actually do. It is an addiction.

Late one evening I got a call from Hamish Black, my old buddy who I had done Kosciuszko with. "So, how do you fancy an adventure?" he said in his broad Aussie twang.

"Okay, I'm listening," I replied.

"Kilimanjaro in two months. I'm going to Africa for a wedding with my new girlfriend and thought we could knock Kili off whilst I'm there."

Sometimes it's funny how your life's dreams take shape. Although Kilimanjaro was on my list, I had no immediate plans, and this random invitation was what really spurred on my Seven Summits challenge. It took me only a few minutes to deliberate and I was in. I needed something to focus on, something to give meaning back to my training and adventure. It was also on my list of Things To Do Before I Die; so for me it ticked all the right boxes. Sometimes that's just life. You hold a vision in your mind for so long, and then the opportunity to do it just pops up out of the blue. The key lesson in life is grabbing those magical moments when they happen and taking action.

So, another great adventure in the making! The plans went pretty smoothly. Hamish's girlfriend (now wife) Lisa had pretty much sorted out the trip and done all the research. She was very organised! All I had to do was get my PA to sort the rest. In fact I had very little to do with the whole process. I just focused on my business as I had only just been away and so needed to get fully on top of things before I tottered off again. I guess I was also slightly sorry for my business partners and wife, so I put myself into overdrive right up to the day before the trip.

In hindsight, I was totally over-confident from the start. (Doesn't that sound familiar?) After the MDS I was invincible, and a long walk up a big hill seemed minor in comparison. And hey, it was Africa, so it must be quite warm too, right? So, all in all, I figured it would be a nice jaunt and another of the Seven Summit scalps. Kosciuszko's easy ascent had also lulled me into a false sense of security as had my good experience in the higher altitude on the Inca Trail. As such, my training was quite minor prior to the trip, just doing a few short runs a few times a week, thinking I still had quite a good base of endurance. How wrong could I be?

Now, because I was so busy and left it to my PA to organise pretty much everything, including my kit, I was very much unaware of what comprised my kit until the last minute. This included the various gadgets she had purchased, including solar power and iPod. This was quite foolish on my part as my PA had never done an adventure before in her life and she was still quite junior. This lack of planning on my side also included a lack of true understanding of altitude and altitude sickness, which was to become my undoing on this mountain.

So what is Acute Mountain Sickness (AMS)?

Most people are aware of the fact that something funny happens to you when you go really high, but few have truly experienced it. And to experience is to believe.

This mountain was to teach me some true lessons on respecting altitude.

As you probably know, altitude is the height above sea level of any point on the earth's surface or in the atmosphere. As you slowly gain altitude, the air becomes thinner, the barometric pressure falls, and as such there is less oxygen available to you to breathe. S. Bezruchka in *Altitude Illness: Prevention & Treatments* puts this into perspective:

Imagine travelling in a modern pressurised airplane at 29,000 ft (8,800 m). If the cabin were to suddenly lose pressure so that the air inside was at the same pressure as the air outside, unless you were breathing supplemental oxygen you would lose consciousness in about 4 minutes and die.

However, Everest at the same altitude has been climbed many times without supplemental oxygen. What's the difference between the two scenarios?

A gradual process called acclimatisation.

And this needs to be done slowly and steadily, 'pole pole'. During this slow, steady process, the body adapts to the lessening oxygen in the air and delivers the necessary oxygen to the cells.

How this affects you as an individual can vary widely, but the common symptoms, all of which I was to experience to some degree in the summits, are:

Breathing adaptation—a need to breathe more, to the point of taking 2-3 deep breaths for each step you take, as each breath is taking in so much less oxygen than you normally need, so you need to breathe so much, much more. It is like running a marathon while breathing through a straw.

- Pulse increase—even your resting pulse is increased significantly as your body is trying to deliver the necessary oxygen to the cells. My resting heart rate (HR) is usually 55, but at an increased altitude it rises to 90/100.

- Sleeping patterns—sleep can be very restless and at very high heights non-existent. Waking to take breaths is common, mainly due to the two points above.

- Urinary response—you need to urinate more, getting up 2-3 times per night to urinate (usually in a bottle in your sleeping bag), at a time when you need fluid the most

- Blood thickens—hence, it can clot more easily

- Vomiting

- Headache

- Loss of functioning of the mind; general decision-making processes become a lot slower and you get disoriented.

Given that little medley of 'fun', it is a wonder anyone wishes to expose themselves to such a game of Russian roulette, and I will have a few occasions where I will doubt it myself.

Altitude sickness is a strange sensation, and having studied it in depth since, there is no correlation as to why, who, and when you may get it. Fitness seems to have no effect. You will see a housewife with no fitness background getting to the top of Kilimanjaro and the paratrooper being wheeled off the mountain. You may get it one time but not another. Our guide on Kili had summited over fifty times, and on the twenty-third he was taken off the mountain in a wheelbarrow. There also seems very little you can do about it, although there is heightened debate in the mountaineering community about a drug called 'Diamox', which is used at high altitudes.

Diamox is a strange drug. Firstly, consider the effects of altitude sickness: nausea, vomiting, headache, unable to sleep. Now consider the side-effects of Diamox: nausea, headache, tingling of extremities, etc. To me it makes no sense, but I did end up trying it much later on Denali and had a very bad night. This knowledge is all great to know now, but at the time of Kilimanjaro, I was pretty clueless and would have to learn the hard way.

C'est la vie. Sometimes we face decisions that have no apparent right or wrong answer, and you just have to choose one and go for it**. It is not about making the right decision; it is about making a decision and making it right.** Sometimes along the way it will become mightily apparent that your decision at the time was the wrong one. Be flexible enough to change strategy and direction based on new facts. Diamox is such a decision — to take it or not? Do not take it and you may be so struck by altitude sickness that you may not make the summit. Take it and the side-effects may be enough to put you off anyway. A later trip on Denali gave real insight into my own personal decision.

Adventure on the way

The adventure really began the moment I touched down in Nairobi, and anyone who has visited Nairobi will know what I mean. When coming out of customs, you are immediately barraged by people hassling for taxis, money, to carry your bags and so on, to which I am not the most receptive. Welcome to Africa. A real jolt to the senses. Thankfully, I had a car ordered, and once I had found my man I felt a great sense of relief.

The car ride was surreal and a real eye opener to the extremes of poverty. I drove past thousands of people in squalor and rags whilst a minute later passing a 5-star hotel. I also had this overwhelming feeling of what it feels like to be a minority. There I was, a Welsh man in deepest, darkest Africa on his own. A humbling experience from the very start and not the last

We finally arrived at the hotel, which was behind very large barbed wire walls and armed guards. Not a good feel, but apparently normal. The hotel itself was lovely—a nice, plush 4-star. The concept of sleeping on Egyptian cotton sheets whilst 50 yards away behind the 12 ft wall people faced abject poverty was troubling for the conscious mind. I have mentioned gratitude already, and I will continue to mention it as it is so important to life's fulfilment. Experiencing and witnessing such poverty does two things for the human soul. Firstly, it drives you to want to help in some way as we are part of a global human family and the distribution of wealth is all wrong. So, it can help drive a philanthropic vision. The second thing it does is give you appreciation for everything you have and how blessed you are. I now sit on the advisory board for Global Angels, a global children's charity, and it has been my humbling adventure experiences that have fuelled this passion. As mentioned in the preface, all author profits from the sale of *Life's Great Adventure* are being donated to Global Angels (www.globalangels. org).

At the mercy of my PA's travel planning, I was now cursing. People were inquisitively asking why I did not fly straight to Kilimanjaro airport, for which I had no answer other than I wasn't aware there was a Kilimanjaro airport.

The next day was another delightful tour back to the airport by taxi. This time it included a run in with the local police/army who stopped the car at gunpoint and, using my driver as translator, tried to extract money from me for no apparent reason. This inbred corruption, despite my nervousness, triggered the alpha male testosterone in me, so I got out of the vehicle and got very mad. I squared up to them, and at 6'4" I was considerably bigger than all the guards put together, although they all had big guns — which really should have been their trump card. I proceeded to rant at them, telling them in no uncertain terms that they were getting no money and to arrest me and get me a lawyer.

I do not think they had seen a mad Welshman in full flow before because despite their having very big sub- automatic machine guns that seemed to get bigger as I was calming down, they backed off. After some exchange between the taxi driver and the gun-wielding authorities, I was told to get back in the car, and we drove off. The taxi driver laughed all the way to the airport. He said he had never seen anyone stand up to them before and they did not know what to do when someone did. When I had calmed down, I had a moment of realisation where it hit me that I had just risked my life for about £5 on principle. The adventure had just begun.

So I embarked on a nine-hour bus ride from Nairobi to Kilimanjaro. Now I don't really do buses in the UK because at my size I do not fit in the seats, and to try to would be my idea of hell. So to be in Africa in a bus in 30 degrees heat would normally be not something I'd consider. But I decided to settle into it and try to enjoy this magical mystery tour, one way or another, keeping my thoughts in check and remaining upbeat and positive.

On the bus there was a menagerie of people from all walks of life. In front of me were two young girls, around eighteen, both Somali and incredibly beautiful. There is something really mystical and wonderful about Somali women. We struck up a conversation and spent the next five hours discussing everything from religion to politics to African rule—a fascinating insight into the world. And to top it all off, one of them was coming to Bristol University the following year. How bizarre. I have to say, by the end of the bus journey, I had a newfound respect and understanding of the Muslim faith.

This is one of the wonderful things about travel and adventure— the insight and perspective you gain of other people, cultures and religions. Wherever I go I am always learning. There is a saying that the human mind works like a parachute; it works best when it is open. I always try to keep open-minded on my trips and gain insight and lessons that I could never dream of.

The rest of the journey blended into the monotony of the magical mystery tour with a stop for souvenirs and to meet local tribesmen, and then the totally chaotic border crossing. Finally, I got to the hotel at the base of Kilimanjaro and checked into my sparse but clean room. I was to find myself appreciating its facilities far more on the way down. It is always a strange transition on adventures. You come from your home comforts and then usually travel in relative comfort to the destination point, with maybe a nice hotel on the way. Then you hit the reality of it all; you are in a tent facing the elements and going to the toilet where you stand.

That evening our group met and had a brief on the journey, a nice dinner and then an early night for all as we made our final preparations for the trip. The group was such a diverse mix, which is also part of a life of adventure that never ceases to amaze me. There was a grandmother, Puran, who must have been in her late fifties and was mother of a man my age; a young Asian lady, Rosina, who had not seen the inside of a gym in her life; two American girls, Lou and Summer; Dante, in her late twenties from Melbourne; Catherine, a red haired oncologist from Canada; Hamish, the rock hard bush walker; his girlfriend Lisa who was also pretty fit; and me. And so the adventure began.

The route in

In the morning, after stashing all our worldly gear that was to remain in the hotel closet, we spent an hour tying down and packing high the fleet of land rovers that had arrived to take us to the base of the trek. And then we were on our way to Kilimanjaro.

At the base of the trail we met our lead guide, Samuel, who must have been in his late fifties. I was sure that when he arrived he was still drunk from the night before. The others, Edwardo, Namen, Nemez and Winiford, all seemed pretty sober though, which was somewhat reassuring. Once again I was amazed by native guides: they seem to be able to smoke and drink, eat anything they wish and still crack on the next day without a care in the world, and with kick-arse speed and resilience. As if on cue, as we set off down the trail Samuel, the lead guide, sparked up his first of many roll-up cigarettes.

Lisa had chosen the Rongai Route, which ascends Kilimanjaro from the north-eastern side of the mountain along the border between Tanzania and Kenya. It has a wonderful sense of unspoilt wildness and was a great choice. We passed through Marangu Gate at 1,800 m in what looked like farmland and began the trek from Nale Moru on a small, winding path through maize fields before entering a forest.

Part of the great diversity of Kilimanjaro is that you pass through and experience multiple landscapes, starting in cultivated lower slopes and moving through Montane forest, moorland, high altitude desert and of course the final mountain landscape and glacier. Each day brings new and beautiful offerings and a mountain quite like no other.

The lower part of the mountain was lovely as we meandered through the lower jungle and greenery. We got to see monkeys and parakeets, and it was generally a good and easy trek. I had decided on this day that I would abide by my old rule from the Three Peaks— you are only as fast as your slowest person—and so I lingered at the back to give a little encouragement to the other members, some of whom were feeling the pace already (not a good sign).

The Rongai Route is somewhat off the beaten track, a little harder and takes a little longer than some other tracks, but you don't have the crowds. Having seen the Coca-Cola Route on the way back down (so named because of all the tea huts along the way where you can buy Coca-Cola), I was very glad we chose the route we did. Kili, I think, is a dangerous mountain for most people. It is one of the few 6,000 m peaks anyone can have a crack at, and a lot of people come totally unprepared both physically and mentally ... as I was about to discover.

The whole lower part of the mountain was a rather uneventful affair, quite relaxed really. And I was holding up pretty well in the altitude. The only things of note that stuck in my memory, and my nose, were the toilets. A lot of people ask, "How did you go to the toilet?" Well, on other mountains it is a different story, but on Kili they have built toilets along the route. So you just need to crouch (or stand) and aim. When I say they built toilets, I mean they have dug very large holes in the ground and put wooden palisades around them, with a wooden platform to stand on with a hole in the middle. This looks all quite civilised, but what you learn on the first trip to the toilet is you need to hold your breath before you go in, and see how long you can survive without air. The stench in these places is truly unbelievable. I nearly passed out on one occasion as I was determined not to breathe for the whole time I was in there.

The true heroes of the mountain

A tale of Kilimanjaro is incomplete without mention of the porters on the mountain. Porters basically carry all the group gear for the trips, such as food, tents and water, and they carry the rucksacks and personal equipment for most people too. These guys are the true heroes on the mountain. Not only do they carry loads, but they are huge loads of up to 100 pounds or more! You can be walking up a trail, feeling a little tired from the day's toil, when speeding past will come a trail of porters, bags over shoulders, some balancing additional bags on their heads and kit hanging from every possible angle. All with torn trainers or flip flops, even bare feet. Incredible. Then when you get to the next camp site, they would have the tents set up, dinner on and a cup of tea waiting, all as if they had just had a stroll in the park. So, to all porters everywhere—I honour you!

On Day 3 we reached 3,600 m and Kikelewa Caves. There the views start to open up and you start to see Kilimanjaro in its full glory; it is a beautiful mountain. In the famous 1936 story by Ernest Hemingway, *The Snows of Kilimanjaro,* he describes the mountain as 'wide as all the world, great, high and unbelievably white in the sun'. I could not put it better myself, although sadly it is less white these days as the glacier is retreating with global warming.

Here is an extract from my journal from the trip, which was very scantly written:

"I am sitting at 3,600 m on Kili. We have spectacular views of the mountain today and it is truly beautiful, magnificent and awe inspiring. It is huge, too! Trekked at a good pace all day, great food and a fantastic team of companions. It is now bedtime and the stars are out and it is the most wonderful sky I have ever seen, so bright, so many and the whole Milky Way, too. Life is magnificent, moments like this are to die for and you really know you are living."

I had really enjoyed my journey so far up Kili. I relaxed and sat back. Sitting above the clouds and looking down to the miniscule world below is a magical experience. I took time to see the sunset and sunrise; both were breathtaking. But, most of all, the stars at night time were just pure magic. I think this is where the real lure of adventure lays, in the reconnection with your soul, the earth and the universe.

The next day was a trek to Mawenzi Tarn Camp (4,330 m), which is spectacularly situated beneath the towering spires of Mawenzi, one of Kili's peaks. Here I climbed up a rock face and sat upon a flat slab for what must have been ages, just looking out over the clouds, soaking in the beauty and energy, feeling truly alive.

This was now the highest place I had been in my life and it felt great.

We were nearly at the summit—Summit Day. We had trekked across on this penultimate day to the final camp at Kibo Hut (4,700 m) across what is called the High Desert. No real events, but the temperature was starting to drop severely and the wind was brewing up a storm. Things were about to get uncomfortable.

Journal entry:

"I am sitting at 4,770m at Kibo Hut, the final base camp, before going for the summit of Kilimanjaro. I am going strong, still no signs of altitude sickness and determined to do this drug-free. All day we trekked high above the cloud line, which was magical, and the final desert plane was reminiscent of the Sahara. I am now sitting in my tent and it is blowing a gale. All wrapped up with every layer I have and preparing for the final push. I am so ready for this now!"

Until now I had had very mild headaches that had gone very quickly, and other than that I had no real symptoms of altitude sickness. So, I was feeling pretty confident and invincible. All other members of the party had had varying degrees of altitude problems, some quite severe, and all were now on Diamox, which was causing its own issues. Summit Day was to push a lot of people to breaking point, including, surprisingly, me.

Summit Day

Yes! It was Summit Day! I was in great shape with no real altitude problems, ready to get this baby done but unbelievably cold. I basically put on every piece of clothing I had in my backpack, none of which was special cold weather stuff. Africa was supposed to be hot, right? I had not even brought a scarf (which only a real idiot would not do), so I cut up a T-shirt I had spare and wrapped it around my neck. I must have looked like a cross between the Michelin Man and a bag lady. All wrapped up at midnight, we set off. Thankfully, it was dark so nobody could see how ridiculous I looked.

Pole pole. I had taken it easy this far as my strategy was you are only as fast as your slowest man/woman. But now I was raring to go. The night was incredible, and I just gazed in awe for the first few hours at the sky and the shooting stars. Being up above the clouds, on a clear night it feels like you are touching heaven itself. But I was getting cold. I don't know what the temperature dropped to that night, but with wind chill it must have been -10/–15, and I was not dressed for it.

'Pole pole' was starting to mean to me 'colder colder', and the group was slowing drastically and suffering. As predicted, two ladies were in serious trouble, and after two major stops to check on them and me getting colder by the minute, I pulled my guide to one side and initiated Plan B—to summit solo. I had already talked to the guide about this before as it was clear a few people were struggling and were unlikely to make it. I thought I would go up with Hamish, but his girlfriend was one of the people in trouble and he made the right call to stay with her. Hence, I was alone. I was like a caged animal and needed to get going as soon as possible.

Now the next bit to any experienced mountaineer who understands altitude was such a schoolboy error. I look back and cringe. But with no experience in altitude, I did not know any better. So off I set, raring to go. The plan: get moving, get warm, get to the top fast. I was given one of the secondary guides, Nemez, to guide me to the top. So, off we bolted. The first half hour went well, and the pace was good and fast. I was starting to warm, and although a headache started to come, I shrugged it off.

Then I had probably the worst toilet experience of my life. Sorry, but I don't know how to describe it in any other way. When mountaineers recommend you buy trousers with moon zippers, which means the backside unzips without taking them down, I now know why. Picture this. As previously stated, I am wearing my entire backpack contents, which includes a layer of skins, two sets of hiking trousers and then wind stoppers over this. I also had big mitts and gloves underneath and lots of layers on top. Very immobile indeed. Suddenly I needed the toilet, a Number Two no less, and all this in -15 degrees on the side of a very steep, very windy mountain at high altitude in the middle of the night. Oh shit! (Excuse the pun.) I tried to shrug it off, thinking I could hold it in, but at such an altitude, when a man's gotta go, a man's gotta go. I pulled Nemez up and tried to explain toilets. He pointed to where I was standing and said to go off the path.

Given it was already –15 and I was already cold, having to drop my trousers and get a breeze up my backside as well was particularly uncomfortable. In addition, I had to take my gloves off, as you cannot unbutton trousers and find toilet paper with your mitts on. Everything seemed to take forever as the Michelin Man/bag lady fumbled his way through the night.

Amazingly, nobody passed, not that I would have cared by this point. But after the event, I was flustered and damn cold. And given future experiences, I now realise how close I was to frostbite. I could not feel my hands at all, and I had lost sensation in my feet and my nose. But we had to keep moving.

Again, we speeded up even more as I was trying to warm up and get feeling into my hands. The effects of the altitude were really starting to kick in properly now as I crossed Jamaica Rocks, the last part of the Kilimanjaro summit path. My head was throbbing, my judgment was clouded and my movements slow and woozy as if I was wading through treacle. I felt drunk and drugged but with a resolute and dogged determination to carry on. Everything was slowing down around me and within me.

I could see what looked like the summit ahead of me, and shortly after I summited the first ridge and reached Gillman's Point (5,685 m). The true top is Uhuru Peak, another 840 ft up (5,895 m/19,340 ft), and the elation at what I thought was the summit was soon popped as I realised we had another few hours to go.

The Death Zone

Mountaineers call the territory above 18,000 ft the Death Zone because human life cannot permanently exist there. The body slowly deteriorates from the reduced oxygen and eventually shuts down. I was now well and truly in the Death Zone and about to appreciate why it is called so.

We cracked on towards the summit, and after about another fifteen minutes of grit and determination, it hit me. I just stopped dead in my tracks, dropped to my knees and projectile vomited three times. Thankfully, Nemez did not see and I just scuttled forward a bit further and dropped to my knees again so that when he came back he would not see the sick, for I knew he would take me off the mountain. I just knelt there, head pounding, stomach retching, wondering what on earth was going on. My mind wasn't working properly, I was slow and confused, and when Nemez started shouting at me (over the wind) to get up and get going, I went to reply and realised I could not actually speak properly. So I just resorted to nodding and giving the thumbs up.

I could see the summit and nothing was stopping me now. I dropped my backpack and clambered around for my water bottles, pretending I just needed a water break. To my utter relief, I found one and put it to my lips in euphoria to take some much needed gulps and clear the taste of vomit from my mouth, only to find it frozen solid. Bugger! So I tried the other, as if in some miracle one would freeze and the other would not.

Nemez just shrugged at me, and I realised I needed to crack on with no more hydration either.

At this point I guess I should have packed up and gone home. But I was young and dumb and bloody determined. So off I cracked, still at a fast pace, as the correlation between going faster and feeling worse still had not registered and would not until I had returned to Base Camp. The next hour was a mix of pain, frustration and … pure bliss. And this is where I experienced first-hand why some of the deaths occur in this altitude.

I was near the top, literally ten minutes away, and I was becoming a gibbering wreck. I needed a rest. I was totally exhausted and really cold but … I just needed a little rest … just a sit down … just for a while. On the last stop just below the summit, the adrenalin was starting to subside as I knew I was going to reach the top. So, I sat down on the glacier, laid back and closed my eyes. Given the external temperature and that I was really, really cold, bordering on frostbite (I still could not feel my hands and my head was pounding), a strange thing happened. A magnificent sense of calm and bliss swept over me, combined with a wonderful sensation of warmth. Nemez was now shouting for me to get up and move, but I just needed to stay ... just another few minutes ... as the bliss and calm set in.

Mmmmmm...

Mmmmmm maybe a little sleep ... that would be lovely... Thankfully, a swift kick and further shouts from Nemez shook me out of my euphoria, and I gathered my focus and rose to my feet. That's when it hit me! I was really in the Death Zone, and death was really quite sweet up here. You hear stories of the bodies found on Everest curled up as if in a deep sleep, and others who have taken their clothes off as if it's quite warm. Although nowhere near the extremes of Everest, that day I had a taste of the sweetness of altitude sickness embracing me, dominating me, and the real danger that lies there — a warning I will carry with me on every mountain.

As I approached the summit, the sun was rising and glistening off the remaining glacier. It was truly magnificent. Shortly after, I summited at 6.30 am. I was at nearly 6,000 m (20,000 ft), the highest I had ever been, nearly 4 miles above sea level. It was beautiful but dangerous; the oxygen up there was half what it was at sea level, and I really knew it. It was like breathing through a kinked straw.

I took the quickest photo that the summit spectacle has probably ever seen and got the hell down. My little nap had really knocked me for six as the true implications of how easy it is to die at this altitude suddenly kicked in. Now I had a very clear and focused plan.

I had just done the MDS; I could run. And I needed to run and get down as quickly as possible. That was all I could think of. I must have been quite a sight as other wannabe summiteers were trudging slowly up the mountain as I, with my Salomon cross trainers, streaked past them at running pace on the way down.

Just above Gilman's Point I met the rest of the team (minus two who were already taken down with altitude problems). They were looking exhausted, apart from the school teacher from the US who looked quite happy and chatty, smiling and taking photos. A world apart from my experience. At this point, I also realised I had streaked a full three hours ahead of the team, and by the time I had finished my ascent it was five hours. I don't remember much of the descent, just the adrenalin as I careered down the scree slopes of Kilimanjaro with no thought for injury, just to get out of the grip of altitude sickness. I got to my tent, to the surprise of the base camp team, collapsed and plunged into a deep sleep, breathing much more deeply again, which is all relative.

The way home

When I woke, I felt so much better. It was like going from breathing through a straw, which was being pinched in the middle, to lapping up the freshest of air through a bucket. And I was still in high altitude comparatively. My water had now thawed in my sleeping bag, and I took a long draught of the freshest, coolest water. Water never tasted so good.

Aaaah. Air and water; what more do you need? Okay, a little food. But to this day, when I am feeling a little down or sorry for myself, I look for things in life to be grateful for and the first things I am grateful for are air to breathe deeply and fresh water to drink. Using a proper toilet is also quite high up the list. So, so many things to be grateful for.

I started to ponder how such a delightful, peaceful trip could have turned to disaster quite quickly and so dramatically, and what to do so it doesn't happen again. Plan the trip myself, be very clear of what I am getting myself into, pack my own kit, know my kit and slowly, slowly, step by step, edge to the summit. Despite being down at Base Camp, the quick soiree with altitude sickness still had a grip on me and I was coughing up blood for the two following days. The memory and respect for altitude and taking things slowly (patience) will live with me for a lifetime.

Journal entry:

"I played the perfect game until I got impatient and went for the summit. An increase in altitude must be taken slowly and patience is key. Also, kit must be the best and you must be prepared for all eventualities. I will know next time."

So, pole pole, slowly slowly. This is probably one of the greatest lessons in mountaineering and one which will pay dividends on future mountains. It is also a great metaphor in life. In this crazy world we live in, the Western civilisation operates at warp speed. We want everything now and yesterday; all our goals need to be achieved in record time. Everything is faster, bigger, better. So, whenever I get caught up in the speed of the rat race, I think, pole pole — the mantra to get you slowly but steadily to where you want to be.

And in doing so, allow yourself the time to enjoy and appreciate the journey along the way. Because I rushed it, I never really saw the high peaks of Kilimanjaro. I never got to savour the summit experience or gaze in awe from the very roof top of Africa. But the lesson is learnt.

Also, invest in your dreams properly. Know what adventure you are truly on and equip yourself accordingly. My ultimate respect goes to the heroic adventurers who first pioneered the great routes in tweeds and hobnail boots. I am no way that tough. The wonder of modern adventure is the kit available, and now I buy the best I can. Never again will I summit a mountain in a jumble of clothes with a cut-up T-shirt as a scarf. So, whatever adventure you are embarking upon in life, make sure you are prepared for it and you invest in it properly.

If I had brought the right kit to the mountain, I would not have got cold. I have been on bigger, colder mountains since and been toasty warm. Preparation is everything. If I had taken the summit slowly, what had been a nightmare experience could have been wonderful. Such is life. You can rush unprepared into situations/events/goals and have a whirlwind experience with a lot of pain. However, with time spent up front planning and preparing, with the patience to diligently execute, you can really enjoy the journey along the way. But, that's a lesson from another mountain.

Time for pole pole, preparation and planning!

TRUE Thinking on

PATIENCE AND PREPARATION

 Shine a light on your Inner Truth

- When was the last time you savoured a sunrise and breathed in a sunset? What about the last time you looked up and appreciated a pure sky scattered with stars shimmering like diamonds? Try it now—go connect in whichever way attracts you. If you are not a country lover, do what inspires you most. If in London, go take a walk up Primrose Hill and witness the magnificence of London.

- Visualise your end goal. Really focus on the feeling it gives you. Define it and get to the source of it. Seek to tap into this every day and feel like it now.

Map out your True Path

- Think now about your goal and what you have to do to prepare fully for it. Add all the small action steps needed to your now building list. Take time and add to it constantly. This journey of adventure and creativity is ever-evolving and ever-expanding.

- Review the time that you have set for your goal. Look now at the things needed to be done for adequate preparation within this time frame. Is your gestation period adequate? Or do you need to give yourself more time? Be realistic but don't procrastinate.

- Create a dream board of your goals and the actions needed to achieve them. Look at all your preparation steps you thought about in the first part of this exercise and put up pictures. Tick them off as you progress, and have fun with it. I had pictures of kit everywhere and ticked each item off as I got them. Don't forget the action bit, though; the dream board without action is a mere whim.

Let your True Guide lead the way

- Think of the synchronicities that have occurred in your life. How did you get that job, meet that person, do that thing? Now, be aware of all the synchronicities in your life every day; expect them and have fun with them. If something goes wrong, like your train is late, maybe it is meant to be to put you in just the right place at just the right time for something magic to happen. Also, be grateful when that occurs.

Magic is all around, but first we need to believe. Then we can live daily in expectation.

- I truly believe the world is constantly conspiring in my favour, even when all the evidence appears otherwise. What do you believe?

Who could support you in your goal? Who believes in you or could believe in you more than you do right now? Who would you like to meet that is an inspiration to you? Do they speak publically; do they have a book or audio? Immerse yourself in their material.

Identify your inner True North

- Get connected to nature. Go for a walk regularly. Spend time with plants, animals, fresh air, whatever appeals to you. Whatever it is, appreciate the beauty and magnificence.

- What can you be grateful for right now? Try to give thanks for at least five things in your life every day. If you are struggling, let me kick you off with some easy ones: your eyes, ears, nose, legs and arms. Appreciation attracts positive energy — the Law of Attraction.

- For mobile users, a great app is 'Gratitude Journal!'

- If you are into meditation in any form, or indeed wish to try, then I encourage meditating on your goal. Listen to the answers that come, the urges, the feelings, and follow them. Ask what preparation is necessary and what should be done next.

Chapter 7

The Alps

PREPARING FOR THE BIG ONES: FACING FEAR HEAD-ON

Our doubts are traitors, and make us lose the good
we oft might win, by fearing to attempt.
~ William Shakespeare

"I was balancing on a vertical ice wall, hanging on for dear life with just the front spikes of my crampons and two ice axes for support. My legs were shaking with the physical hardship of it; every muscle was burning. Or perhaps the shaking was partly the fear again; I could not tell anymore.

My mind would not work. My heart rate was soaring. Sweat was beading and dripping from my helmet as the sun blazed and reflected off the pure white glacier into my eyes. I gingerly removed one ice axe to reach higher and hammered it in as deep and as hard as I could. As I tried to pull the other axe out to match its brother, the ice beneath my feet gave way, and suddenly... I was falling."

Following the experience on Kilimanjaro, what was next? Quit? Believe you me, I thought about it. But, thankfully, I now had the bug for adventure and my long-term vision and passion were firmly embedded, even if belief was knocked a little. 'What's next?' is a big part of the comedown of any big adventure or addiction in life, and I suppose adventure is my crack habit. I can think of worse, though! By the time I had touched down at Heathrow from Nairobi, I had decided that Elbrus in Russia would be my next peak and my next of the Seven Summits.

This time, however, I would be prepared. Learning from the debacle on Kilimanjaro, I bought mountaineer books, researched the web, and contacted numerous guides and companies to set up a thorough plan for the next big adventure. Lots and lots of little steps forward toward the ultimate goal. I quickly discovered I was entering true mountaineering territory that involved glacier travel, crevasse rescue, ice axes and crampons. So, time to get serious and time to get trained.

This is a normal part of any great adventure where you reach a point where you are well and truly outside your comfort zone and beyond your skill and ability.

Every great master started somewhere. Leonardo had to learn to draw; Beethoven had to learn to play. I had to learn to climb.

So I picked what looked like one of the best guiding companies for Europe, IMS, and proceeded with my plans. IMS were great and based in Wales, so all my conversations with them were laced with the lovely lilt of the Welsh accent, which made me feel much more at home. What I learnt very quickly was that I needed the right kit and to practice on a glacier before I would be ready to go to deepest, darkest Russia. Trouble was there are not many glaciers in the Forest of Dean.

Facing my fears, ones I did not even know I had

So, I picked the closest and cheapest option, the Alps, on an intense glacier and mountain training program.

I thought this trip would sharpen my skills, build my confidence, and ensure perfect preparation and planning for Elbrus. To my surprise, it would have the complete opposite effect. My confidence would plummet, and I would have to face some huge fears head-on, fears I never even knew I had.

Before we head to the Alps, let's talk about fear.

It is said we are only born with two fears: the fear of falling and the fear of loud noises. The rest we create for ourselves and pick up along the way. There are many different scales of fear, from slightly fearful or nervous to terror. Everyone has different fears in different degrees. It is how we deal with these fears that define us. At that point in my life, I can honestly say I did not have many real fears, and I could actually say I was quite fearless. I think rugby taught me a lot here; getting bashed about every Saturday hardens you up a bit. But this is not such a great trait to have because if we are not feeling just a little fear along the way, perhaps we are not stretching ourselves enough. I was guilty of not stretching myself and reaching for my dreams. So, I was about to discover real fear the hard way.

In some instances, fear can actually stop us from even starting something. We have to deal with our fear head-on before we make any progress—so we need to deal with it now. In other cases, part way along our journey fear will creep up on us, or we may be faced with a fearful situation that is unexpected. There is fear of failure, a common one, which holds many people back, and there is its archenemy, the fear of success, which appears an oxymoron at first glance but is very real indeed.

Let's talk about the fear of success. This is something I have had to battle with in the world of money and business. If people are very settled into a community, family or social scene, to actually succeed in something amazing could have an ostracising effect. I've heard of a type of syndrome that best describes this effect, which is known as the 'crabs in a bucket' syndrome, though I'm uncertain of the source. Essentially, when you put a load of crabs in a bucket (think people in a group), if one tries to crawl out, the others pull him/ her back down. The net result: no one escapes. If only those crabs worked together, they could get the whole team out. Something to think about.

I was reading the newspaper whilst writing this (yes, men can multi-task, too) and as if by magic (there is that magical coincidence again) there was an article on fear. It listed the **Top Ten Most Anxious Moments of Fear**:

1. Giving birth/attending the birth of a child

2. First day on a new job

3. Marriage

4. An operation

5. Buying a home

6. Losing your virginity

7. Redundancy

8. Meeting the in-laws

9. First kiss

10. Leaving home

I found this fascinating as at least seven, maybe ten, depending on your perspective, are all key moments in life that could be massive, positive and life-changing moments for the better. Yet fear is associated with them all. And that is the irony: fear and success are very closely related, and most of us on our journey need to overcome fears at some point to savour true success and fulfilment. As you will find when you read through this book, I have looked fear in the eye many times on my adventure, literally shaking in my mountaineering books ... and I still continue to do so every day. It is a necessary part of life.

When did you last fail?

As mentioned earlier on, I was very blessed early on in my career to work for one of the greatest companies in the world, Mars Inc. Yes, the chocolate giant and multi- billion dollar food powerhouse. What is particularly special and unique about Mars is it is still a family- owned company and hence encourages family values, which includes risk and growth. During one of my very first appraisals in which I was expecting a pat on the back and a glowing report, my boss (Stacey Wallace) asked me a question that totally stumped me: "When was the last time you failed in the job?"

My answer, after slight silence, confusion and delay, was that I had not. To which she retorted that I could not be trying hard enough or pushing the boundary enough. I was gobsmacked.

I don't think I took in the lesson fully then. In fact I was a little miffed. Stacey did say I was her biggest challenge; I never was very malleable. That lesson lingered with me for years, and to this day I thank you for that, Stacey. And it is so true. If we are really living life, going full out and pushing the very boundaries of our potential, by default we will fail at times along the way. So, I ask you, when was the last time you failed? If it was not for a long time, then maybe you are not pushing your boundaries enough.

Another article again this month in SUCCESS magazine pointed to the **Six Deadly Fears of Entrepreneurship**:

1. Fear of failure

2. Fear of inadequacy

3. Fear of risks

4. Fear of financial insecurity

5. Fear of what others might think

6. Fear of growth

This is a great article, and you can almost take away the word 'entrepreneurship' and apply this list to most areas of life. Somewhere, sometime, you are going to have to deal with fear. So we might as well start to deal with it now.

I was at a local county show recently where they had the Paratrooper Tower, a recruiting mechanism for the Paras[4]. Basically, you climb a big tower and jump off vertically. I have already faced my fear of heights head- on (as you will see in the Alps), so this would not have phased me. I could have done it for a bit of fun, a quick hit of adrenaline no doubt, and with some nerves, I am sure, as I approached the edge. But that

---

[4] British Parachute Regiment

would be about it. To somebody else, however, this could be a major life event, possibly facing a lifelong fear of heights. As I stood there watching, I noticed a man who had just come off. He was in his sixties and was absolutely beaming and proudly wearing his new Para T-shirt. He started telling everyone what he had just done and that at sixty-five he still had it in him. He was so proud, so buzzed and his self-esteem was boosted massively. He had faced his fear.

Curing your deeper fears

If your fear is deep and ingrained, and there is nothing you can do to remove it, then there is plenty of external help. I am trained in NLP (Neuro Linguistic Programming), and during my training I was curing phobias. What amazed me was the pure range of phobias and fears people had and more amazingly the speed in which they could be 'cured' with the power of the mind. I proceeded to work with my partner, Sylvie Gourdon, who had a fear of spiders, and within thirty minutes I had her holding a tarantula — quite a shift!

I must say, I should have had some work done on me because by the time I had finished with her and she was holding the tarantula, I think I was more scared than she had ever been.

But despite all this, I have seen numerous instances where fear was not overcome and phobias not cured. So, what defines the difference? I believe it is to do with how much the person really wants to overcome it. Of course, some fears are there to serve us, like the fear of falling or heights.

So if your fears are deep, challenging or emotional, I strongly urge you to seek out a good NLP coach or hypnotist who can work through some phobia/fear work with you.

Time for the next adventure to begin. I am off to the Alps, with proper kit this time.

First, the kit

The first thing I needed was a pair of boots, but not just any boots; I needed super boots! After my cold feet on Kili, there was no way I was doing that again, and I needed boots that would serve me on Denali, Aconcagua and Everest. Wanting and finding, however, are two different things. Thankfully, after much research I discovered one of the best adventure shops and advice centres in the UK—Snow Rock and Ice, Covent Garden (www.snowandrock.com). An adventurer's dream! This is to me what TK Maxx is to my wife. But most importantly, the staff is just superb and knowledgeable, in particular a guy called Rory.

Thanks, Rory.

So I bought all the kit. The boots alone, Olympus Mons, cost a mortgage payment, but I was determined to be ready for whatever the mountain threw at me. With crampons, ice axes and all the bells and whistles that come with mountaineering, I was now ready and raring to go, and realising this is an expensive sport if you do it right.

Let the experience begin

When I was planning this trip, one of my business colleagues and a close friend at the time, Rohan Weerasinghe, started to show a real interest. I think his recent fortieth birthday had given him a midlife adventure kick. So he decided to join me. This was fine, and although he had no altitude experience or endurance experience, he was quite an accomplished rock climber. So his skill on ropes and rock was excellent whereas mine was zero.

The only problem with this set-up was Rohan's preparation, or slight lack of it. I had learnt this the hard way and Rohan was soon to have a similar lesson on Elbrus. Rohan is one of the finest minds I know and a great speaker. His abilities in positive thinking and mind over matter are legendary, though I think probably a little too strong at that times, as his fitness regime prior to the mountains was a little under-adventurous. He somewhat underestimated the challenge on Elbrus.

The other issue was we were friends and in business together, and challenges like this really push you to your limits and can strain and stretch relationships to the max, maybe break them. Nevertheless, to the Alps we went.

The trip over was pretty uneventful. We spent the first night in a lovely chalet nestled in the side of the Alps. It was September, so the weather was nice and it was off- season from skiing, so the place was pretty quiet with only a few rock climbers and mountain bikers. The guide arrived the next morning on cue. He seemed nice enough and clearly very experienced, so off we went for our first day. The goal for this trip was to gain in five days all the key skills that were required for Elbrus and Denali. So we started off with ropes and crevasse rescue.

Despite my pre-training with some ropes and basic knots, boy scout style, for some reason the knots proved most problematic, and whilst Rohan was knocking them off like some swotty boy scout on speed, my efforts were looking more like a rat's nest. After several hours and considerable boredom and frustration, I think the guide and Rohan gave up on me and accepted that my knots would just have to do. I just really hope I never need to do a crevasse rescue otherwise the one to be rescued will be in a little trouble and would be better off trying to dig themselves out with a spoon.

So onto rock climbing. To this day I still don't know the relevance of the next skill for my mountaineering other than to frighten the daylights out of me and nearly put me off mountains for life.

We firstly embarked on a one pitch climb, which basically means you climb vertically as far as one rope can take you (I am sure the technical climbers out there have much fancier terms, but that was what it meant to me). Now, I wasn't built for climbing vertical rock faces, and to be frank I really never want to do one again. But in the spirit of things, I cracked on and did what was expected. I knew one pitch hanging from your toes and fingernails was doable, and if I fell it was only for about 20 ft, so I wasn't going to die. I tried a bit of abseiling, and although there were a few arse- twitching moments, it again was doable. Following this it was time for lunch, a wonderful Swiss lunch with cheese, olives and fresh bread.

The three pitch climb

So far, so good. Pretty crap on the knots, but I can get better. Pretty rubbish on one pitch climbing, but I did not see the relevance anyway, though this was disputed by the guide and Rohan. I decided, however, to drop the argument even though I felt I was right. I had done my research on Denali and knew someone who had climbed it who did not mention vertical climbs. After lunch we embarked upon even more rope work, and then the guide decided in his infinite wisdom that we were now going to do a three pitch climb. He again insisted that this was indeed required (which, now having done Denali, I would vehemently argue against). But, once again, I sucked it up and just got on with it. What harm could it do anyway? Rohan was also goading me on by now, as he was in his element. He was scaling the rock face like Spider Man and using his historic skills and his very slight build, which allowed him to hang effortlessly from cracks.

The first pitch was fine, but that was the end of what I would call fine. Looking upwards at the second pitch, I could see a little pair of legs disappearing around the rock face directly above me. This was what can only be described as a place on earth where man was not meant to travel. I looked upward in a perplexed, slightly nervous fashion, wondering how on earth I was supposed to climb that. After a mixture of hanging and crawling, grabbing and shunting, I very un-stylishly got to the top of the second pitch. I was puffing, blowing, sweating and now quite fearful. Several times I thought I was going to fall and die! Then I would look up and know with certainty that I was. Up to this point I had faced nerves and scary moments, but now I was really looking true fear straight in the eye.

The third pitch was vertical and smooth. There was nothing to hang onto and scurry up. It was a flat wall to me, not even a slug could have got up it. As I assessed the impossibility, I heard shouts from above from Rohan and the guide, who had been chatting away together quite merrily at the top, telling me to hurry up. I know what I wanted to tell them and where to stick their ropes and climbing shoes, but a final taunt of "If you want to do Denali, you need to be able to do this," was the straw that broke the camel's back. I cannot say what I was thinking at that point, as it was X-rated, but up I went.

Now, I think climbing usually looks like a graceful, spiritual quest, one of intensity and sublime focus. But mine was in rage, fear and pure gutsy determination. Unfortunately, that doesn't always work. Half-way up, when my anger had subsided, I found myself hanging by the fingers of one hand, with the toe of one boot stretched across the rock face desperately seeking that something, that anything, to put either a finger or a toe on. In fact I wasn't being fussy — any protrusion right now would do for a nose, ear, knee… I did not give a shit as I was now panicking. The language in my head, and now externally, was blue. The guide lent down over the ledge above and said, "Don't worry. If you fall, it will be fine. The rope has you."

I was hanging by my fingers, hundreds of feet from the ground in the midst of the Alps, and what do I do? The one very stupid thing that every film, book and adventure TV show tells you *not* to do when at a great height: look down. I stared a hundred feet down to jagged rocks and felt what it was like when people joke about their sphincter muscle twitching. That was it. I was here on some stupid mountain, sprawled vertically across a flat rock face I really shouldn't be on, hanging by my fingertips, and I am going to fall and die. And just to make matters worse, I was probably going to shit myself on the way down and die humiliated.

Now my legs were turning to jelly and my left leg started to shake uncontrollably. All I knew was that every ounce of my body was telling me it absolutely wasn't okay to fall, but if I do fall, I will die.

Remember the two fears we are born with—fear of falling and a fear of loud noises? Well, I was about to face both; firstly, the fall, and then the loud bang when I hit the floor. And in my head they were both very, very real possibilities.

The next few seconds felt like hours, like days, as I finally surrendered to the inevitable. Nothing in my rational mind could accept that falling was an option. The ingrained, natural response from birth was telling me that falling, and from this height, was a death sentence. I was paralysed with fear and indecision. In the end, gravity forced the next move as my fingers and toe were slipping and could not hold on any more.

I glimpsed a tiny ledge a few feet away—when I say ledge, I mean tiny crack—which was made for pigeons with very small toes. I swung, let go and grabbed for it. That moment of release, where for a split second I was several hundred feet up and nothing was holding me up but will itself, was terrifying. It seemed like everything slowed down, and strangely a feeling of liberation became equally evident.

I was facing one of my greatest fears and surrendering to it. I wasn't conquering it or smashing through it like I was used to doing. I wasn't controlling the fear or defining it. I was simply accepting it and releasing into it. For the briefest of moments, I was free.

I got to that ledge and several more equally … and finally I was at the top. My heart was racing so fast. I was wet with sweat and weak with the sudden expenditure of adrenaline. I was so elated … and so angry! Before I could catch my breath, gather my thoughts and punch the guide, both he and Rohan leaned back over the ledge whilst discussing something or other, and told me to come on down when I was ready as they abseiled off.

I was furious now and exhausted. After a few minutes of calming myself down with some deliberate deep breathing, just being thankful I was alive, I finally started admiring the wonderful scenery ... until a horrible sensation hit the pit of my stomach. I leant over the edge to see the guide 100 ft below, roping. *I an't abseil! I've never abseiled before except for that piddly little practice just now on the one pitch climb. And after what I've just been through, now's not the time to start. F****

I spent quite a while on that ledge figuring out how to abseil and picking up the courage to face another fear so quickly after the most traumatic moment of my life to date. But having already faced possibly my worst fear, this one seemed strangely more acceptable. Ultimately, I did come down and vowed never to do that again.

I can now look back and laugh at this, even if it is nervous laughter still. Time is a wonderful healer and can give wonderful perspective. At the time, though, things could not have felt worse. I was literally scared for my life, and it ruined the next few days and cast real doubt on my future mountaineering.

So, what did I learn by looking fear in the eye? Well firstly, if I had just learnt to fall/fail a little bit first, I would have been much more comfortable with falling higher up. I had never fallen, so I had never learnt to trust the rope. I have since been told by a climbing instructor that the first thing they do with children is get them to fall first from a few feet to get used to the feeling of falling and to know and trust the rope— such a great metaphor for life. We need to get used to failing, just a little bit every day, every week, so that when we face bigger obstacles, we can face them with more certainty.

The other big lesson for me lays in the question: Was the fear real? Now, if you had asked me at the time, I would have vehemently answered, "Absolutely". But looking back now, logically and non-emotionally, the fear was indeed in my mind. The rope did ultimately have me, but I did not trust it. Sometimes we need to step into the fear and trust.

Glacier travel the hard way

We spent the next few days high up in the Alps in crampons using ice axes and practising rescue techniques. We climbed a peak opposite Mont Blanc, which was wonderful, but the following day was tough. I was wearing crampons for the first time on a glacier and getting used to ice axes and using them to stop falling in what's called an 'ice axe self-arrest'. (My lack of skill in this would come back to haunt me on Denali.) All of this was new and uncomfortable, plus my confidence had taken a real knock. The haunting from my rock climbing experience had stayed with me. Once one's thinking becomes so negative, it pervades everything to follow.

Having found my feet on the glacier and become used to traversing slopes and some technical ice fields, the guide in his infinite wisdom struck again as he had us attempt to scale a vertical ice wall. This time I kicked back and argued vehemently against the necessity.

And again the 'If you want to climb Denali card' was played. So up I went. Now, my ankles have always been my weak spot, having broken them both playing rugby, and balancing on vertical ice walls by the front spikes on your crampons is not a great ankle exercise. I struggled massively.

But up I went as I tried desperately to complete the challenge. I was balancing on a vertical ice wall, hanging on for dear life with just the front spikes of my crampons and my two ice axes for support. My legs were shaking with the physical hardship of it; every muscle was burning. Or perhaps the shaking was partly the fear again; I could not tell anymore. My mind would not work. My heart rate was soaring. Sweat was beading and dripping from my helmet as the sun blazed and reflected off the pure white glacier into my eyes. I gingerly removed one ice axe to reach higher and hammered it in as deep and as hard as I could. As I tried to pull the other axe out to match its brother, the ice beneath my feet gave way, and suddenly ... I was falling.

Thankfully, I was only about 6 ft up, so the landing wasn't too rough! That put an early end to my glacier traversing for that day, which I was eternally grateful for.

Although crashing into the glacier below wasn't death- defying, I did sprain my ankle and all in all it was another huge blow to my already shattered confidence on the mountain.

Recovering from fear

The whole experience in fact shook me up for months, and it did not help that my climbing partner and friend, Rohan, kept on at me that if I could not do vertical climbs and abseil, then I would struggle on Denali. He just wound me up more and more. Anyway, I figured Elbrus was to come first and wasn't too technical, so I would do that and take it from there. Interestingly, the tables were about to be turned.

Sometimes you need to look fear in the eye like I did on that rock face and glacier in the Alps. Once you have faced your fear, you can then decide if you really want to proceed and do it again. I have learnt to accept my fear, and to me it is perfectly acceptable now. The fear I experienced, the fear of falling, was totally natural and actually there to serve me. Having a healthy fear whilst hanging from a precipice is natural, and it is the fight or flight response kicking in, trying to protect.

Some fears are like this, like a healthy fear of spiders, snakes and sharks as they can all kill you, as can falls from heights, fire and so on. So take a look at your fear and see if it serves you; it may be a protection mechanism. If your fear is irrational or you cannot see a way in which it serves you, then you need to deal with it before you can move forward.

I was to face more fears on Elbrus, Denali and Aconcagua, but for now I was pushing the limits of human potential and that is where fear lies. I would learn to deal with fear more over time and accept it as an ally not an enemy. I will also learn to listen to it, not merely smash through it as so many gurus advocate.

Sometimes, by merely breaking through, you do not listen to the true calling of your soul and learn the real lesson along the way. Fear is there to serve us and to hinder us. I would rather keep my enemy close to me and make it a friend.

And so I would carry fear into deepest, darkest Russia where I was about to face my first true mountaineering test.

Time to learn to deal with good ol' healthy adversity!

TRUE Thinking on

DEALING WITH ADVERSITY

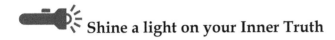 **Shine a light on your Inner Truth**

- How do you really feel about your fear now?

  Write it down and get clarity on exactly how the fear makes you feel. Work through whether the fear is rational or not. A fear of public speaking is incredibly common. If that is one of yours, go to your local Toastmasters and get involved. I have seen some incredible transformations at Toastmasters where people have faced their fear and won.

  If you continue to really struggle with a fear that you wish to shift, I would highly recommend seeking out a good NLP practitioner, coach or mentor.

Map out your True Path

- What fears do you have about your current goal/situation? Are these fears reasonable or fact-based? Can you alleviate these fears today by doing something, facing something, perhaps getting more accurate information? If so, do it.

- Map out what you are going to do, get clear and just do it anyway, despite any fears. Think how great you will feel having faced your fear and looked it in the eye. This builds massive self-esteem instantly. Feel the fear and do it anyway; you owe it to yourself.

Let your True Guide lead the way

- Write down a time you can remember when you were really scared or got completely out of your comfort zone. Describe the thoughts and feelings before, during and after the event. Use these as memory joggers:

  - Fear of failure

  - Fear of inadequacy

  - Fear of risks

  - Fear of financial insecurity

  - Fear of what others might think

  - Fear of growth

- Visualise what it would feel like not to have these fears. Describe how your day would be, how differently you would behave.

- Believe in a life where you face your fears with confidence.

 ## Identify your inner True North

- This is a great time to meditate and reflect on your fears, in whatever style you prefer.

  Listen attentively to what your body is telling you. Perhaps it will tell you that the fear is to support you. Use your meditation to get clarity.

Chapter 8

Elbrus

MAKING TOUGH DECISIONS

Everyone who has ever taken a shower has had an idea. It's the person who gets out of the shower, dries off, and does something about it that makes a difference.
~ Nolan Bushnell

"Balancing on the very edges of my crampons in the middle of the scariest ice climb of my life, I looked up to a crevice we needed to surmount. My heart sank. I can't climb that! I can barely balance where I am. I would now have to clamber vertically up an ice face to reach the ropes above. All the fears of the Alps came rushing back, all the doubts crept in. But this time it was for real; this was no practice. I was 18,000 ft up one of the most dangerous mountains in the world. My mental resolve was collapsing from within. The shouts of the guide hovering above on the glacier were mute as my internal battle raged. I went to reach for a grasp but it was too far. I looked for another way; there was none. I needed to take a leap of faith; the fear gathered momentum inside."

It took me months to recover from the Alps as I had a lot of internal battles to face from my experiences. In fact I did not really put this behind me for many years. However, like most fears, sometimes you just need to get back on the horse, if indeed you decide you ever want to be on a horse again. Believe me; I really questioned my future mountaineering at this stage. Thankfully, my vision still burned inside for the Global Grand Slam despite this setback. Elbrus was the next logical step to really discover if I could face real mountaineering.

I had all the kit from the Alps and had already agreed with a provider on costs, so it was just down to booking it. I did so a few months after returning from the Alps, allowing several months of preparation, mentally and physically, before the big test. Rohan was now all fired up about mountaineering after his successful trip to the Alps where he excelled at everything. I guess that's what frustrated me the most. It was my dream of the Seven Summits that Rohan had piggy backed off part way through. Even more annoyingly, he then excelled at everything whilst I just could not get it together. Even the ropes and knots I still could not get my head around. My whole thinking had been sabotaged internally, and my greatest strength in mind control was rapidly turning into my biggest enemy.

This is the great dichotomy of the mind, which I would liken to a garden. As a passionate gardener myself I fully appreciate this metaphor. You can clear a full garden patch of weeds, painstakingly removing the rocks and twigs, and then plant that garden with beautiful flowers. Then if you leave that patch unattended for a long period, it is just a matter of time before the weeds take over and choke the flowers. And you are left once again with a patch of weeds and grass.

This is just like the mind. I spent years clearing out bad thoughts, nurturing good thoughts, thinking positive and reframing my thinking. After the Marathon des Sables and Kilimanjaro, I got complacent and stopped nurturing a little; I stopped weeding. Then my trip to the Alps was the equivalent of throwing a big handful of rocks and weed seed all over my patch. By the time I was ready to do Elbrus, the patch was weeded again, not fully, but partially.

This involved a lot of self-reflection, taking apart each mini disaster and putting it all back together again; understanding why I failed so miserably and then stepping back up one small step at a time to face each fear. I did a lot of meditation during this time too, really assessing whether this vision was indeed the right one for me, as I really had not enjoyed the Alps and I was supposed to be doing this for the passion and love of it. After much reflection, I decided I needed to give it one more go, to see if this mountaineering thing was indeed the passion I believed it was; one more roll of the dice. And if I hated it, I would then turn to find another hobby. So, my destiny in mountaineering came down to one big mountain, in deepest, darkest Russia.

Journey to Russia

Not many people realise that the highest point in Europe is actually in Russia—Mount Elbrus. Many believe it to be Mont Blanc in the Alps—a beautiful and very accessible mountain. But, unfortunately, to step further towards the coveted Seven Summits, a much longer and more remote trip was required.

Mount Elbrus is based on the Caucasus Main Range on the border between Europe and Asia (though there are differing views on how the Caucasus is actually distributed between Europe and Asia). The Main Range is a state border between Russia and Georgia. It is a volatile zone to say the least, which explained the many gunshots we heard along the journey. The summit is a mighty 5,642.7 m with the saddle elevation at 5,416 m, and believe me that last 200 m is felt every step of the way. It is a little lower than Kilimanjaro, but this lesser height is more than made up for by the more technical nature of the climb as it is mostly glacier and snow work and a lot colder.

It was quite a challenge merely getting to Elbrus. Following a decent flight to Moscow, the transportation got shabbier as the journey progressed. The flight from Moscow to Mineralnye Vody was comical. The plane was like something out of World War II, and the airport terminal we arrived at was a glorified tin shack. We then sat back in a ramshackle minibus for the four-hour drive from Mineralnye Vody to Azau.

What strikes you immediately this deep into Russia is the poverty all around, a different poverty to that of Africa, with a very different energy. It is quite hard to explain. I liken it to a sadder poverty—many grim faces, a sadder, stricter, straighter energy, one where fun has been removed. This was in strict contrast to areas of Africa where the poverty was far more extreme, yet the children would be running down the street laughing and playing. It was a particularly thought-provoking time for me as I had never experienced or witnessed communism at work.

We arrived at the hotel, which was basic to say the least, but the people were lovely. The communication was somewhat challenging this far into Russia as very few people spoke any English. Thankfully, we had the lovely young daughter of the hotel owners translating for us. The biggest issue on this trip from the very beginning was food, as we were both at this time 'Fegetarian' or 'Fegan'; we did not eat meat or dairy, but we ate fish. Trying to stick to just eating fish in these parts of Russia wasn't the best decision as we were miles from the sea. So the next week or so meant more cabbage than I would like to remember.

The next day the guide took us on an acclimatisation trek from Cheget. Given my 'pole pole' experience, I was taking this very easily. But Rohan was like a mountain goat and was striding ahead, keeping a really fast pace. I warned him about 'pole pole' and the difference in heart rates at different altitudes. But he was adamant that he was fine, so I let him go on. Altitude sickness is impossible to describe unless you have experienced it. I began to think that here we were again; Rohan the overachiever was going to be miles ahead of me for the whole trip.

We climbed to about 3,100 m that day and, although not easy, it was thankfully not too strenuous. The journey had begun. It was such a secluded place and the scenery was just wonderful. We also got our first glance at Elbrus itself, and it was massive.

The next day we began our climb properly. We took the ski lift up to The Barrels, aptly named as they are literally huge, round metal barrels that have been turned into huts. They are a bizarre collection that makes this first part of the mountain look disturbingly industrial — like an oil refinery. We trekked in with full packs to the base hut, Diesel Hut, which sits at 3,800 m. Again, Rohan had been streaking ahead. I was determined not to get competitive. It is so easy to get wrapped up in someone else's pace and to compare ourselves. I had learnt by now to only compete with myself, all part of my spiritual gardening. I listen

Deri Llewellyn-Davies

to my body, and at that altitude you need to listen even more attentively as there can be such subtle shifts.

Already the effects of the altitude were starting to kick in. On Kilimanjaro you have several days to slowly acclimatise to such a height, but this climb had involved quite a quick jump in altitude from near sea level to 3,800 m. Luckily I was armed with the experience of Kili. I had learnt to drop the ego and not compete, maintain my own pace and conserve my own energy. This would prove to pay dividends, but in a way I would not expect.

Settling into Base Camp

Diesel Hut would be home for the next few nights. We would acclimatise here and use it as Base Camp. We were to take several acclimatisation trips from here, going higher each time, and then after about a week we would attempt to summit from this point if all went according to plan.

The hut is a strange combination of part-chalet and part-garden shed, balancing precariously on a rock face on the main glacier face. It is like a massive garden shed inside packed full of small wooden camp beds.

It is aptly named Diesel Hut as it smells constantly of fumes with all the cooking going on at all hours inside.

Despite my experience on Kili, the altitude gain here was too quick and my resting heart rate went through the roof, to the mid–nineties (normal is mid-fifties), and as such I could not sleep much that first night.

Despite my best efforts and learning to take it easier and slower at this altitude, I would find this mountain needed to be

167

approached in a very different way. But that was okay. We were supposed to just spend time at the hut getting acclimatised, as well as taking further intermittent trips up the mountain. So, there was plenty of time to get my body used to it—a whole week in fact.

But sometimes even with the best laid plans fate takes over. My plans were about to fall apart in a most spectacular fashion.

As we settled into the hut we got talking to the other climbers and found that a number of teams were going down from the mountain, somewhat disillusioned and broken. The weather, it turned out, had been so bad they had been hanging around for a week with their failed attempts at the summit, and they had had enough. Plus the weather signals for the next week weren't looking any better, in fact worse. Not good. And as if to prove the point further, I went for a look outside and a storm had come in so hard I could barely see past the front door. It was my first experience of real cold and the harshness and danger that mountaineering can throw at you. Thank God we were in a hut, not a tent.

We settled in for what might be a long and frustrating wait. Welcome to real mountaineering. Looking on the bright side, I now had a few little friends to share this experience with as the hut was infested with mice. Well, they were either really small rats or really big mice. There I was in the middle of the night, resting heart rate 96, wide-eyed and unable to sleep, just lying there with my mind whirring. I decided to have a little snack, so I got some nuts out and placed them by the side of me. At some point I drifted off into a little doze but was awoken by a rustling and nibbling noise. When I opened my eyes, there right in front of my nose was a bloody great rat-mouse-thing, sitting there eating one of my nuts. I think in any other time or place I would have probably screamed like a girl and ran, but for some surreal reason it all seemed okay, and I just dozed off again. This altitude plays funny tricks on you, and this would not be the weirdest one on this trip.

The next day as we took a trek in full ice gear up to Pastukhov Rocks at 4,700 m, we started to experience altitude sickness. Again, Rohan went ahead like a bullet from the off, and again I let him go. As we were approaching the rocks some hours later, I was appearing to be rapidly catching him up, and I wasn't really going very fast. In fact I was slowing as I was so determined to maintain a slow pace — 'pole pole'. By the time I reached the rocks, I knew why I had caught up; Rohan was in trouble. The altitude had finally got him, and it had happened suddenly and dramatically. Just like me on Kilimanjaro, his speed had accelerated the onslaught. He was in a bad way, and we needed to get him down — fast. The weather had also just turned bad. We came down in a total white-out, barely able to see in front of us. For the first and only time, I needed to use my altitude meter and compass to get my way back to base safely.

Rohan was very shaken up by the experience, and now he was showing altitude symptoms proper. It would take hours for him to get remotely back to normal. I left him to settle for a while as the only thing to do now was to wait. And we had a week to work it out.

Hopefully, he would recover in time and maybe make another attempt at an ascent. Otherwise, he was off the mountain. As for me, I sat back, listening to the storm howling in the background. I decided to re-read a book on how to acclimatise on Elbrus, as this could be a long wait.

Gut-wrenching decision

About an hour after our fateful return, the Russian guide came up to me looking troubled, and in broken English he said we needed to make a decision. He had been on the satellite phone downstairs, checking on the weather patterns, and debating for some time with other guides. The weather was bad, had been bad, and was likely to continue to be bad. But there was a sign that that night there could be a break in the weather in the very early hours, and that could give us a slight chance to give the summit a shot. If we did not try, we may not get another chance and may have to go back down due to weather.

Oh, crap.

Now this was a tough decision on many fronts. Rohan was nowhere near up to it; he could barely make it to the rocks that day, so a summit attempt straight away was out of the question. As for me, so far I felt good, apart from a high resting heart rate and little sleep.

But given my experience on Kilimanjaro, I knew I wasn't acclimatised and did not want to screw another summit up. To add fuel to the fire, this was a very dangerous gamble because if the weather did come down on me anywhere near the ferocity raging outside whilst I had altitude issues, the combination could be fatal.

But … if I did not take this chance, I might not get another. Crap. So do I:

- Go for a summit attempt with Rohan, knowing that he is likely to not make it, meaning we all have to come down?

- Go for the summit alone with the guide, leave Rohan behind and take a risk on altitude sickness myself as I am not acclimatised?

- Not go for the summit and wait to acclimatise properly, and just hope and pray the weather forecasts are wrong and we get another break in weather? If not, we go home with no attempt.

- Be done with it? Rohan was rough, and maybe it was time to come off the mountain.

Decisions in life, particularly big ones, are rarely one- sided. Usually some sacrifice is needed, or there are pros and cons to weigh up that could swing either way. And that is just a part of life. Sometimes you make the right decisions, sometimes you don't. When you don't, you learn from the inevitable fall-out. Just try to ensure you don't make the same mistake twice, and move on.

So, what did I decide?

I asked the guide to give me time to think it through and discuss it with Rohan. I could not face Rohan yet, though, and I needed some air. So I pulled on my boots and my down jacket and ventured out into the storm, pretending I needed the toilet, which, as it so happens, I did.

It was just the distraction I needed as I battled through the storm to get to the external toilets: two little huts balancing on the edge of a rock face. I wrenched open the door against the wind and battled my way inside. I took a deep breath of relief to be out of the storm and then nearly passed out as the stench from below hit me. I looked straight down a hole in the floor to a sheer drop of 40 ft. At the bottom lay years of excrement. I felt my gag reflex as I nearly puked down the hole. The rest I will leave to your imagination, as I am gagging with just the memory.

After a very quick toilet stop, as I could not face the stench, I battled my way back to the hut. I sat out on a ledge, sheltered from the wind, to stare into the eyes of the raging storm. It was pure, whitish grey in all directions, serene and fierce at the same time. I don't know how long I sat there, but I tried to clear my mind, connect and meditate to give me some perspective. In those moments, I found a little peace, which is what I needed to make a decision.

When I face a big decision in life, I ensure that no matter what, I take the time out to calm my mind and meditate to find the answers and then to reflect on the answers that emerge. It has never failed me.

I have sometimes failed myself by overruling those internal, peaceful decisions with logical, thought-out ones. But I can honestly say that without fail those internal decisions are always the right ones, and now I trust them fully. On that day in the depths of Russia, I did not yet have full trust in my instinctive, internal decisions, but I was about to find out if the decision I chose was the right one.

Ultimately, I thought I had a shot and this might be my only shot. I had to take it or I would regret it. Rohan had partly caused his own issues because he would not listen and attacked the mountain too hard, just like I had on Kilimanjaro. I went in to tell Rohan the situation, and we had quite an emotional exchange. I really felt for him as this was his dream too. And I felt totally selfish in that moment. I was to learn that mountaineering is selfish, as is life sometimes, and it is a sport that centres round summiting, no matter what. And here I had to leave my partner behind in the hut whilst I attempted the summit. Thankfully, in the end, Rohan understood; after all, it was his exuberance that had been his own downfall. Still, it was so hard leaving him behind.

It was now late, and there was no point in going to sleep. So I just started to get my kit on and prepare for what I was about to face. I was fully kitted out and just lay on my bed, mind whirling with thoughts. As I lay there and glanced to a rustling on my right, there was my friend the mouse-rat who had come to see me off.

And he had brought his mouse-rat wife too. How nice. Each of them had a nut as if to celebrate my decision… a decision that I was starting to doubt.

It was only Day 2, and I was already going for summit. Everything I promised I would not do after Kilimanjaro was now coming back full circle to bite me. I thought about my fateful summit in Africa and was scared about facing that again. I spent most of the night wrestling with my doubt and fears.

Due to the very short window of opportunity, six of us were going to make a summit attempt, and as such the guides hired a big snow cat for 3 am. So, in the middle of the night, after two nights of no sleep and in a weird mix of exhaustion and exhilaration, we trekked out to the snow cat. I remember walking out of the hut in a hugely sub-zero temperature of -30.

As I went out of the door, I looked up to see a clear night sky. No pollution, full of stars and a full moon— it was just magical! The night sky and sunrise on the mountains are my favourites. What a massive transformation from the raging storm merely hours before. I will learn that these extremes in weather on mountains are normal and deadly. Things can change in a heartbeat.

The snow cat emerged out of The Barrels below, two huge eyes beaming light up the mountain, its roaring engine the only surreal sound in an otherwise peaceful night. It crept its way up the mountain very slowly, battling against the deep snows that had been laid down by the storm.

When it arrived, we all clambered onto its back and held on tight as it propelled its way hundreds of meters up to the fateful rocks where Rohan had seen his highest and last point on Elbrus. Now I was already feeling the altitude as this was a risky strategy. The snow cat got us the head start we needed to capitalise on the small window of opportunity, but that meant we were being thrown higher into altitude quickly, without giving the body a chance to acclimatise.

Tossing all my 'pole pole' lessons to the wind again.

To make things worse, the moment we got off the snow cat, my guide set a blinding pace as he wanted to get up and off the mountain quickly, so he decided to break trail. What that meant was that with loads of deep snow on the mountain from the storm, there were no clear paths or trails to follow, so we would need to make our own. Up to knee deep in places, this made the climb unbelievably difficult, with each step a battle. It was a huge physical effort.

The trek to the summit began in earnest. I was trying to keep a steady, slow pace but my Russian guide was pushing me a lot, and I knew why. We really did not want to be caught out here. I was struggling, and my internal self-talk was starting to take over, warning of the dangers of the altitude and that following Kilimanjaro this was not part of the plan. Thankfully, I had my music to distract me. But after one hour of music, which had been the key to fuel my motivation, my iPod died a death due to the altitude (older models do this), and I had only myself to talk to for the next eight hours.

I was fixated all morning on the summit I could see in the distance. Step by gruelling step, ploughing through the snow as we inched our way upwards. For hours on end nothing was said, and we just continued in silence knowing the risk we were taking. Half-way up, the sun rose slowly over the Caucasus, and it was magnificent.

I stopped briefly to catch my breath and to truly absorb the sunrise; the magic and the beauty were overwhelming. I looked back for the first time in hours to see that we had blazed a trail and lost everyone else by doing so. I was alone on the mountain with my guide. From this vantage point we could not see The Barrels or the hut, or anything else for that matter. It was just me and the whole mountain range at sunrise— one of the most magical moments of my life. But I did not have time to continue to appreciate the view and the moment; we had to keep moving. So, the guide shouted something in Russian, which I guessed meant get your arse in gear, and the moment of solitude and beauty was shattered. I needed to remember where I was and how dangerous it was. Nevertheless, the energy of the view fuelled me on for an hour.

We carried on for hours, and I threw every last piece of energy and determination at the summit I saw ahead.

It wasn't much further. I knew I could do this. The exhilaration was building, despite the exhaustion in my body, as I knew I would soon conquer Elbrus…

Then my euphoria was totally broken in an instant … I finally came over the ridge I had been so fixated on, only to see a saddle and a much bigger mountain looming ahead. Crap. It was a false summit.

The final push

The mental setback of thinking you have reached a goal and then realising you have not reached it at all is crippling. I had thrown every last piece of energy at that false summit. I dropped to my knees on the saddle; I felt I was in pieces, with no gas in the tank. Thankfully, the guide had also decided that this was our first real rest stop and had dropped his kit and wandered off to dig a toilet hole, as he needed a Number Two. That gave me the time I needed to have a real word with myself internally and try to pull myself together.

I lay back in the snow, the sun shining down on me now, blinding me and warming me. The extreme cold of the night was slowly ebbing away. *What was I to do?* I had come this far. The weather was holding out, but I was cooked. The altitude was taking effect now, and I knew what it was doing from my experiences on Kili. I was in a really dangerous position, and my mind was starting to play tricks on me. I looked upward towards a summit I could not yet see, and the size of the next climb overwhelmed me. It was also the steepest section I had ever seen. The thought of balancing precariously up this glacier on my crampons would have scared me on a normal day. But this wasn't normal. I was already totally exhausted, with now massive altitude problems.

So, again, what to do? I lay back and meditated on the answer. Firstly, my resolve stated I had to give it a full go. I had come this far, and I needed to give it my all, although I already felt I had given it my all. The sight ahead was overwhelming, so I needed to use the tactics of the MDS and just pick off a small section at a time. I held the purpose of the Global Grand Slam in my mind, the vision of summiting, all my fears, my learnings and the decision I had made earlier.

It is such a difficult call on a mountain, unlike a marathon where you just give it your all until you cross the finish line, and then you are done. Mountains are much more calculated. When you do reach the summit, you are actually only half-way, so you have to learn to preserve your energy, which is a very difficult balance.

Despite this, there was also something else missing. Something extra was needed, and it needed to be beyond myself. In a flash of inspiration, I decided to dedicate each little section to someone I loved, past and present, and to do it for them. The first section would be for Rohan as he would have given anything to have the chance I was facing. And so I set off.

The final two hours to summit were a real, real slog for me as I took one small step after another, drawing on every last piece of strength in me. I experienced real gratitude and flashbacks of all my loved ones as I focused on each one individually as I climbed each section, from my wife to my dead father. I turned what was undoubtedly one of my greatest physical challenges into a profound and quite spiritual experience. And most of all, I prayed and gave thanks.

After several hours, we came over a ridge and there before me was a plane of totally untrodden snow, gently rising to a summit cairn[5]. There lay the highest point in Europe, one of the coveted Seven Summits — and my third.

I lumbered across the plane, swaying now like a drunken man with the effects of the altitude seeming to flow through my veins like some good Scotch whiskey. I reached the summit, dropped to my knees and prayed with tears in my eyes. The moment was so profound. My guide sat a little bit down from the summit in silence as I just stood on this highest point, taking in the full 360 degree panorama of Europe's highest point. I had the full mountain range and full scene all to myself. The risk had paid off. The decision had been the right one.

The euphoria of summiting was amazing; my first proper one. And unlike Kili, I was determined to savour the moment — to drink it in. But we were only halfway through our day's journey, so the savouring moment had to stop. We had to head back. The weather was starting to change again, a sign that we needed to get down fast-and fast we went.

The descent was rapid and a total blur. I was drunk on the altitude and riding high on adrenalin from summiting. I think I surprised even the Russians in how fast I descended, using my favourite tactic learnt on Snowden — the rapid descent. I did, however, have a little wake-up call. As I was ploughing my way down the glacier, my guide shouted to stop and pulled

---

[5] Cairn is a term used mainly in the English-speaking world for a man- made pile of stones. The cairn is to mark the summit of a mountain.

me up. When I looked at him questioningly, he just casually pointed about 4 ft to my left to a tiny crack in the snow, below which lay a gaping crevasse. I learnt to take my time and respect descents a little more after that.

The gut was right

As we approached the hut, we found Rohan waiting, and we embraced. There were no words needed between us; we both knew how tough my decision and his had been. I knew absolutely now that the decision had been right. Given how tough I had found it, and I had previously been okay on this mountain, Rohan would have definitely had to come down. That would have ruined my summit attempt. I thank him for his selflessness on that day, although I know it hurt him.

We all face decisions along our journey, many, many decisions — some easy and some hard. The hard ones are usually the ones that define us if we have the strength to make them. Sometimes you have an opportunity presented to you, and in that fleeting moment you need to weigh up the pros and cons and make a call. That call is often the difference between achieving your dreams and not achieving them.

Therein lies the power of a decision, and sometimes you just need to go for it.

Very rarely, if ever, are things perfect. The people who wait for perfect situations and events very rarely accomplish anything. You have to just take the best odds, reduce the risks and go for it. I used to be very logical in my decision making, but now I like to take a balanced approach. When it is possible, I like to take time out to meditate and reflect internally on the decision.

I have honed this ability over many years, and now I trust my gut totally. It is rarely wrong.

I have, however, had many gut feelings or hunches that could not really be explained in a logical context. The facts and logical evidence pointed clearly to one decision but my gut to the other. In times past, I have overridden my gut, and every time I did I was proven wrong. On Elbrus all the evidence pointed to wait, acclimatise and then maybe, just maybe, we'd get another shot. My gut told me to go for it, and this time I did. My gut was right.

So, make a decision and make it right. If it doesn't work out, don't be stubborn. Recognise it was the wrong decision and choose another. Admit when you are wrong, learn the lessons and move on; don't dwell on it. You will soon find that I was about to make a very wrong decision on one of the most dangerous mountains in the world.

On my return, and with added confidence, it was time to take on 'The Big One' ... Denali. Otherwise known as Mount McKinley, it is the highest peak in North America and situated in deepest Alaska. Little did I know why they call it The Big One and compare it to Everest. I was about to find out.

Time to learn how to make tough decisions!

TRUE Thinking on

MAKING TOUGH DECISIONS

 Shine a light on your Inner Truth

- If you had to dedicate your goal to someone, who would it be and why? How can you serve whilst achieving your own goals? So many people do marathons and sporting achievements on behalf of a charity or a loved one. There is a huge reason for that. By going beyond and serving other people, we serve ourselves. Think how you can serve more by achieving your own goals.

- If you make your decision and it turns out right, how would you feel? What if it goes badly? How would you feel? Choose your feelings wisely and focus on the good feelings every single day.

Map out your True Path

- Think of a tough decision you need to make. Now weigh up the pros and cons. List them fully. Weigh carefully the balance between the two; sometimes the choice is obvious, sometimes not. Is there anything you can do to reduce the cons? If so, do it. Really spend time on this and write down even the most obvious.

- Ultimately, you need to make a decision. If you have not got enough information, then go get it and try again. If you are still languishing, then meditate on it or go to a quiet place and follow your gut instinct. You will usually be right.

- Remember, not making a decision is making a decision.

Let your True Guide lead the way

- Think back to the time when you made two separate tough decisions, one that was right and one that was wrong. What does your 'gut' feel like with each decision? Do you get the 'I knew I should have done that' feeling or 'I knew I shouldn't have done that' feeling?

  Really feel the difference. NLP practitioners can help you tune your awareness as can many spiritual teachers.

- Can you think how achieving your goal will positively impact others? In your decision making, think about the wider effects on other people. The ripples you create in your decision making may go far wider than you first perceive, for good and for bad.

 ## Identify your inner True North

- Instinctively, what activities do you think you will find the hardest to do in following through on your decision? Where will you face the obstacles? Plan to overcome obstacles before they even occur. I do this with my clients all the time. We get clear on what we would do if a certain event happened. Then if by chance it does, no panic, we deal with it. Make sure you implement a reward-based system for these activities particularly.

- Learn to meditate on your decisions. Tune into your inner voice. Learn to know which one is right as there are several voices inside us; don't be fooled into thinking they are all right.

Chapter 9

Denali

DEALING WITH FAILURE

Failures are like skinned knees, painful but superficial.
~ H. Ross Perot

"*The fever was returning and getting worse. We were of course gaining altitude and my chest was being punished simultaneously. I was coughing more and more until it was a hacking cough, and I was bringing up phlegm. Then about forty minutes before Base Camp, I suddenly felt as weak as a kitten and collapsed on the ground.*

Everyone else went on. I was left in tatters with just one of the guides. I continued at a crawl. My chest was rattling as I coughed up more phlegm and spat it into the wind. It was nearly 4,000m and I obviously had a chest infection. Next to a broken leg, this is the worst infliction you can have up here.

Slowly but surely I got to Base Camp that day... The diagnosis was not good: deep bronchial chest infection, high fever (40 degrees) and high blood pressure, all of which are disastrous at this altitude. Was this attempt over before it had even begun?

I was euphoric after my summit on Elbrus, and this success had negated a lot of the doubt and fear from the Alps. All the skill and technical ability of Rohan had not helped him one jot. On Elbrus stamina and ability to deal with altitude were primary, as was mental resilience on Kili and the MDS. In hindsight, though, my euphoria was lulling me into a false sense of technical security. I probably thought I could conquer anything now!"

Time for one of the big ones

Now things were going to get a little more serious, as the next peak was to be Denali (Mount McKinley to some). Denali is one of the toughest mountains out there, even compared to the Himalayas. Being in deepest Alaska and bordering the Arctic Circle, it is notorious for its coldness. Part of myth and legend on Denali is the Denali Pass, a saddle just below the summit. This is one of the most inhospitable places on earth as it creates a natural venturi effect that doubles the wind's velocity as it blows through this tiny pass from the western extremes of Siberia and eastern Russia. Legend has it that people have been literally flash-frozen with the extremes this pass has to offer.

Not the most compelling holiday blurb I have ever heard. In time, I was to discover the true viciousness of that pass. It is a memory that will live with me forever.

This, like the MDS, requires a full medical certificate. My doctor, Dr King at Drybrook Surgery, chuckles whenever I come in as it is never because I am ill, but for some new 'event' I am off on that I require signing off for. I also had to go through rigorous due diligence with the guiding company as this is not a mountain just anyone is allowed to enter. Experience and skill are necessary. All my previous summits and experiences accumulated to give me just the level required, and I mean *just*.

Post-Elbrus I was on a high. Through my successful first three summits of the Seven Summits, I had progressively built my skill and experience. I was now ready for the next big one, or so I thought.

Up to this point in my life, I had been flying along at full speed in all areas, accelerating in my career and business growth. I had had a huge business challenge many years earlier, nearly threatening bankruptcy, but I overcame that to prosper. I had built many businesses. I sat in executive and non-executive positions on multiple businesses and had a large property interest. I was married, had several houses and had just had my first child. So life in all areas was good. But all of this started to crumble pre-Denali with the onset of the recession and the crashing property markets. The months prior to Denali were challenging to say the least, both professionally and personally.

As a result of this pressure, my fitness wasn't great and nowhere near where it should have been for Denali. But I was under so much stress at work, and had so many balls in the air, there was no other option. I had trained as much as I could, but was confident enough that my muscle memory and previous fitness levels would be enough to carry me. But I also had huge personal reservations about going; I faced a lot of self-doubt. My business partners were 'anti' because of how much was going on back at home. I was facing financial ruin. Really, was this the time to go off exploring?

But, the whole trip was already paid for and non- refundable, as was the kit. All I needed to do was turn up. Everything back home was a mess, and deep down I needed to run away to reflect. And that's what I did. I needed time out to reconnect, to figure out what next, to face my fears. Financial ruin was my biggest fear, and I needed to deal with that. Solitude in the depths of Alaska would give me the space I needed.

Hence, I faced Denali with a lot on my mind, not in the right mindset at all. Combined with my limited fitness, all this would stretch me to my absolute limits.

I was about to really discover the power of the mind and how it can truly affect the whole of you in all areas of life simultaneously. You cannot be miserable and down in one area of life and not let it transcend across everything else. Your thoughts and your mind are all pervasive, and bringing this negativity with me to Alaska would prove nearly fatal.

My departure was not great. My business and financial pressures had put a large strain on relationships, and I parted on pretty bad terms. In hindsight, my decisions were selfish and a bigger man would have stayed, but again this was one of those tough decisions that had no right answers, and my gut was telling me to go. This bad farewell would haunt me for the whole trip. I had a long 24-hour journey to get me into deepest Alaska. Plenty of time to think through a lot of stuff, clear some negativity and get my mind ready for the trip.

Flying into Alaska

After a rather long journey into Alaska, I arrived at Talkeetna where the journey was about to begin.

Talkeetna is one of the quaintest towns I have ever seen; it looks like a picture postcard from the last century, virtually untouched by Western influences. I loved it. The hospitality matched the picturesque view, and the traditional food on offer was a delight. On the way back down from the mountain, I recall thinking that this food tasted like heaven itself.

After a day of full kit check and meeting the team, we were good to go. It was an all-American team, run by RMI, an American company who proved to be an excellent outfit. So I was the token foreigner, which meant that we spent the next month goading each other fully. The team was strong and diverse, but unlike with other mountains, everyone here was a seasoned mountaineer, and I was about to find out why.

The start of the trip was incredible as the only way onto Denali was by aeroplane — a very small 3-seater to be precise. The plane was packed literally to the roof with all our bags, packs and equipment. Then, with full kit, we squeezed into the seats with our knees up to our chins. In jumped the pilot, and then we were off with no messing around; windows of weather to get on and off the glacier are few and far between.

We had an incredible forty-minute flight over some of the most beautiful Alaskan glacier terrains and mountain ranges. I flew in with Walt, a senior exec at Microsoft, and my tent buddy for the next month. Suddenly the mountains opened up and we dropped out of the sky, landing gracefully on an open stretch of glacier dotted with tents — the first camp. We exited very swiftly, dropped all bags, picked up sledges and got out of the way so the pilot could get airborne again and get the rest of the team.

And there we were, having been literally dropped into the middle of the Alaskan mountain ranges, miles from anywhere. It was unbelievably beautiful. The views on the day were incredible, a total panorama, and I just sat and watched in awe for some time. It felt good to be away from the real world and all the pressing problems. I felt the freest I had for months.

That was where we were to sleep that night as it took quite a while to get the full team on the mountain and the weather had started to change. We put up tents, had dinner and that was us on the glacier. We practiced a few ice axe self-arrests, and we learnt special slip knots to put the tents up and, more importantly, how to secure a tent to ice – a very different tactic. That is probably the most amazing thing about the Seven Summits: the pure diversity of every mountain, so different to each other yet equally beautiful in their own magical way.

Walt would prove to be one of my greatest tent colleagues of any of my trips. He was the epitome of what you would need: thoughtful, hard-working, diligent and calm. All of these traits would prove invaluable in the coming weeks.

So the next day we started the trek into Base Camp, and I was buzzing. With full pack on, which was quite heavy at 40+ kg and dragging a sled of team equipment behind me of equal weight, I felt invincible as we glided down the slope and onto Denali proper. This was what real exploring was all about; this was going to be the biggest adventure yet.

The downhill turned to uphill quite quickly, and that did not change for the next three weeks. Within two hours, I was totally knackered and was calling on every last bit of reserve I had to get me through the first day. This was going to be terrible, and I wanted to go home. Imagine this, you are carrying a full pack on your back, weighing 40+ kg, and on top of this you are dragging a sledge behind you with another 40 kg in it, all up a very big hill! No, up a mountain through snow and ice. And it is cold, very cold. I wasn't fit enough, and I knew it.

I have never been happier to make camp as I did that day, until I discovered the reality of making camp in Alaska. You get in to camp, and then the work begins. You have to stamp out an area for the tents in the snow as the ground is all soft snow. Once you have stamped an area, you pitch your tents in windswept and freezing conditions, securing them to the ice with huge stakes and ice axes. With tent up, you need to dig a hole for the vestibule to put your boots and bags in, digging down with picks into the ice. And then after a full day's trek and hours of work, you think you are finished, but the work has only just begun.

Then you have to cut blocks of ice, as big as a microwave oven, out of the glacier landscape and build walls all around the tents to protect them from the vicious weather. You then have to dig out a kitchen and build walls around that too. Finally, a quick dinner and bed. OMG. This was excruciating, and I realised I had to do this every day for the next month!

Now just when you think this experience doesn't get any worse, try doing it all in permanent daylight, even sleeping. Alaska boasts 24 hours of sunlight as the sun doesn't set in the summer months, and that plays havoc with your body clock. But that night it did not bother me. I just pulled a shirt over my head and slept like a log, albeit a very cold log.

The next few days were similar, doing the whole routine again, building each camp each time, the only difference being that the slopes were getting steeper and steeper. Soon we were in crampons going up scary-looking ice slopes whilst still dragging our sleds.

As well as building tent walls at each campsite, we built walls for the kitchen tent and of course the toilet. I got right into the building after a while, and my creations got more and more elaborate, including crafting a fine toilet at 14,000 ft which had its own toilet roll holder and urinal. I spent many a happy and proud moment in there.

Yes, let's talk about the toilet. Believe me, going to the toilet in Alaska is somewhat of an experience, one that is incredibly uncomfortable and defies common sense. But you could not do Number Ones and Number Twos together; they had to be done separately. You'll soon find out why. Each camp had a few pee holes that must have gone down 100 ft. This was always a major scare factor because if you fell in, imagine it … death by pee hole! Tragic. But Number Twos were done in a purpose-built little bucket called a 'can' by the guides.

Imagine a typical bucket at home, reduce the size to one third, the size of a child's beach bucket for sandcastles, and there you have it. Lay a plastic bag inside, and that is your throne. Then you attempt a Number Two in the bucket once you have stripped all your layers down. You freeze your behind whilst also trying to hold in your Number One to do later in a pee hole. How I never wet myself on Denali I will never know. I think if I did, I would not tell you anyway.

The reason your Number Ones cannot go in the plastic bag is because all poo (frozen) goes back down the mountain with you. You can imagine the weight if you have to carry down your frozen pee! Hence, the pee hole and pee bottle. I discovered the delights of the pee bottle fully, which was my saviour in the tent. I would, though, learn that you need to make a clear distinction between your pee bottle and your water bottle in the middle of the night in your sleeping bag, where they were all stored.

The climbs were pretty scary, with some steep sections where we were balancing precariously on our crampons. It would not have been quite so bad if I wasn't dragging a 40 kg sled which kept sliding off the paths, trying to drag me down with it. The slog continued to High Camp where we remained for a few days to acclimatise. And I spent those few days staring up at where we were to go, half in awe and half in terror. In the next stage of the climb, I was to experience being the most scared I have ever been, surpassing even the Alps.

Facing old fears: the vertical glacial climb

The next day we set off pre-dawn and weaved up the mountain in a zigzag fashion. The slope got steeper and steeper. Just sitting to rest involved digging in with ice axes and securing yourself. This was real mountaineering, and I wasn't sure if I liked it. I knew the fixed ropes were approaching and I was praying for the stability they would bring.

Balancing on the very edges of my crampons in the middle of the scariest ice climb of my life, I looked up to a crevice we needed to surmount. My heart sank. *I can't climb that! I can barely balance where I am.* I would now have to clamber vertically up an ice face to reach the ropes above. All the fears of the Alps came rushing back, all the doubts crept in. But this time it was for real; this was no practice. I was 18,000 ft up one of the most dangerous mountains in the world. My mental resolve was collapsing from within. The shouts of the guide hovering above on the glacier were mute as my internal battle raged. I went to reach for a grasp but it was too far. I looked for another way; there was none. I needed to take a leap of faith; the fear gathered momentum inside…

I panicked. I could hear the team behind shouting me on as I was in their way whilst the guide from above was shouting as well. I really did not give a shit about any of them. It felt like the Alps again. As the rest of me froze, my legs started to shake again, only this time it was imminently more dangerous. It was a mix of fear and anger that got me over that ledge, and I still do not know quite how I did it as I think the fear wiped my short-term memory. The next thing I do remember was being attached to the fixed rope above and giving thanks to God. My heart was pounding; sweat was dripping off me as the heat from the sun started searing from the glacier. I looked up. It was now almost vertical. I still had a long way to go.

The fixed ropes are there to support you, and you use an ascender to get you up. It is like a one-way handle that you can push up the rope but won't slide down. So the climbing began, crampon driven into glacier, next one driven in, ice axe secured, ascender moved up. I would repeat this routine hundreds of times. Finally, we came over the top of the vertical ice ridge that we had been climbing for hours. And I was knackered, physically, mentally and emotionally.

We were only part way there though. I then had to navigate further steep ridges, culminating in several ridges a foot wide (my boots are a foot wide) where down each side all you could see were several thousand feet drops. And the guide was shouting back, "Don't look down." Yes, thanks, very helpful.

Finally, we reached the point where we were to cache our gear. The profile picture on my Facebook page was taken at that point. The scenery was amazing but the experience was terrifying. That moment for me defines where I overcame my fear the most, and to date was the biggest physical and emotional challenge I have faced.

The heart-breaking thing was we had to go back down to do it all again the next day. The next day, though, I went up and I actually quite enjoyed it. I knew I had done it once, so I could do it again. I had broken down a huge barrier in my fears, and now I revelled in the experience. I was admittedly exhausted, but the fear had gone.

This is such a key lesson in life. I could have given up at any point, and believe you me I wanted to. I was terrified in places, but I just kept taking another step, trusting it would be okay. Once I had done it, I had stretched my fear to a whole new level, and now I would face Denali or any other mountain of similar grade without fear — always with respect — but not fear. You have to face your fears head-on by just doing them and doing them again; it's a repetitive process. You fear, you try, you experience, you try again, and so on until the fear is gone or you choose not to continue.

So I had reached 17,500 ft and had conquered a lot of fears. I was knackered, really knackered, but ready. The summit was almost in sight. This was to be home for the next week. We made camp, built walls and built some more, just to be sure, and then got ready for our summit attempt. At this height, I built the best toilet yet and spent a lot of time playing cards. I was also able to use the satellite phone more and connect with home. This wasn't the best as things were going from bad to worse at home, and I ended up having to have several legal conversations at 17,500 ft with lawyers as the harsh realities of the ruin I faced back home came flooding back. The doubts came with them, and I plunged into a deep depression.

Going for the summit

Then, on the third day in High Camp, we decided to go for it. The summit gear came out, as did the nervous excitement as we prepared. The day was beautiful, and we started off really well. It was tough and getting tougher as the effects of the altitude were really kicking in; but so far so good. I just wanted to get it done now and get off the mountain, as I had not been in the right frame of mind from the very start, and even more so now since those phone calls. We were about one hour from Denali Pass when the weather started to turn.

Denali is so massive that it has its own weather front that can change in a heartbeat. We cracked on, but my kit was starting to let me down. It was incredibly cold now at -30/-40, and I was losing the feeling in my hands. This was giving me even more problems because I needed to hold an ice axe and a walking pole to keep me on the mountain. Then things got worse, dramatically worse, as my goggles froze over and I was suddenly blinded. It happened in minutes.

So, there I was on a particularly steep bit of glacier, balancing precariously on my crampons, using my ice axe to support with hands I could not feel, and I could not see anything. Things were bad, really bad. I tugged the line to the guide and shouted out my predicament. I don't think he could hear me, and if he did, he did not care. He told me to just keep going as we were nearly at the pass. So I did, each step a guess as to whether I was on the right piece of glacier, whilst trying to get feeling back to my hands. This went on for thirty minutes. The weather was now howling, and I could not see anything. I had experienced something similar in the Sahara with sandstorms, but now this was the opposite: cold, claustrophobic and frightening. Each step a gamble.

We got to Denali Pass and the whole team was in tatters, not just me. The Denali Pass was proving its notoriety; it was like hell unleashed—a very, very cold hell. This storm was the worst I had ever experienced and I think ever will. It was a whiteout. Whilst I was worried about my own predicament and 'blindness', other members of the team were far worse off, suffering from the first signs of frostbite. We needed to get off the mountain and get off fast. So we did. The guide checked over everyone. I explained my situation, got my hands moving again and cleared my goggles.

And off we set. Within minutes my hands were numb again and my goggles frozen, and this time we were going down and at pace. To make matters worse, the guy in front had the worst signs of frostbite on his face and had panicked, so he was setting a blazing trail down. Since we were roped together, he was pulling on me, me who was blinded and could not hold the ice axe properly. Not a good combination.

I stumbled blindly through the blizzard and down the glacier, guided only by the tug of the rope, each footstep a gamble. It was like playing Russian roulette with each step, and I felt my luck was running out. As we descended, I started to lose the feeling in my face too as the cold bit in further.

I was on the very edge, literally, as we tried to make our way back along a tiny glacier edge. I blindly took one more step then there was suddenly nothing below me. I felt a split second of weightlessness, of peace … and then I plummeted into the abyss. Below were thousands of feet of pure glacier and certain death. Realisation kicked in fast, adrenalin faster still, as I thrashed wildly to do an ice axe self-arrest, wishing dearly that I had paid more attention in the lessons and practiced more on the baby slopes. I slid now, picking up speed down the side of the glacier, shouting to my comrades who I was roped to, praying one could hear in the din of the raging storm all around.

All lessons in ice axe self-arrests at that point were thrown out the window as I thrashed wildly to try to get my ice axe, pole or crampon into the hard ice below. All the while I was shouting "Fall!" which was the technical term, but I think it was more like "F***!". Thankfully, my guide did a perfect self-arrest and I managed to get something anchored as I came abruptly to a halt ... and hung there.

Everything was quiet apart from the beating of my heart, which sounded as if a drum was being played outside of me. The faint sounds above were muffled in the rage of the storm as I came back to reality. There were shouts now to get moving and get back up to the path line. I looked up through my blinded goggles. I could not see anything but knew I needed to go up, so I did. One crampon at a time, ice axes hammered into pure ice as I started to scale the glacier. I had fallen about 20 ft, but it felt like 200. I was exhausted. I could not feel my hands, and I could not see. I continued the climb up, kicking in hard with crampons and powering the ice axe in taking no risks. Pure adrenaline got me up. And then we went off again, stumbling into the white abyss. I fell two more times before we got back to camp, and two of the team came down with frostbite. A brutal day on the mountain.

Stripped to the core of my being

About 50 yards from camp, whatever adrenaline had kept me going wore out. I collapsed to my knees and just stayed there. The guides tried to get me moving, and I abruptly told them where they could go.

I eventually made it back to the tent, got into the sleeping bag and got the life back to my hands and face. I have been eternally grateful for my hands and nose ever since. We take them for granted, but how precious they are to us.

The next few days as we recuperated I had to do a lot of soul searching. The team was preparing for another summit attempt, and I needed to decide whether I wanted to be part of it. I was still ruined from the first summit bid. The businesses were in free fall back home, accelerated now by the banking collapse. I surely faced financial ruin on my return. I had been broken on that mountain and in life in general, and there was no fight left in me. In truth the lack of fitness had paid its toll, and although I had one summit bid in me, I did not have two. And we still had a long trek off this big slab of ice to go.

I remember standing on a huge rock precipice, looking out over the Alaskan Range at a view that was breathtaking. I was really done. I had really hit an all-time low in life. I had never really failed so dramatically in any huge area of life, and here I was with my life collapsing around me on all fronts— business, financial, relationship, fitness. And now, the one thing I had always been successful in, my adventure, I was facing failure in too.

All the fight was gone now. I was completely stripped of ego. I let it go. I had nothing more to prove. It was me and the mountain. I looked down and had a fleeting thought of ending it all. I had huge insurances against me, one step and it would all be over. It was dawn and no one was around; it would be put down to a mere accident. My wife and family would be covered and financially free. Just one step ... This, after all, would be a magnificent place to die, quite fitting really.

When all is said and done, I think it is love that is all that matters, unconditional love. Because of my financial ruin, I had ruined my love relationships too. Because of my selfishness, because of my greed, I had let it rule my mind and my thoughts. But, without this love, what was the point? I felt I had lost the love of my wife and my mother, and this way I could put it right. Financially.

I looked down, lifted my boot and took a step. This was it; it was for the best. Maybe now they would see I was always doing it for them and was prepared to pay the ultimate price. In that moment I released everything.

I had faced all my fears and now nothing else really mattered. I was at peace. Nothing could touch me as I faced death. I had looked death in the eye and smiled back.

Then the one true love, the one unconditional love I had, flashed across my mind—the love of my beautiful daughter Aarrowen. She did not care about the money, business or stress; she just wanted her daddy. She just wanted my time and my energy. That was all, no conditions. If I was to do this now, I would leave her growing up without a daddy, even though she would be financially free. I could not do that to her. Suddenly money became irrelevant; there was a price I wasn't willing to pay.

I stepped back, took a deep breath and thanked God for the life he had given me to this day. I prayed, thanking him for the blessing I had in my beautiful daughter, and that I loved her beyond words. The words of an old mentor came racing back to me: True wealth is what you have when all your money is taken away. And now for the first time, I truly understood that. I had my health; I had my hands and nose. I had a family that loved me, a beautiful daughter who loved me unconditionally. I had family and friends; I had all my experience and education; I had my memories; and I had wealth beyond words. And I did not need to summit to prove anything. I did not need financial success to prove anything.

So I stepped back and retreated to contemplate in my tent. I decided not to go for summit again. Again my gut made the decision and again it was right. My fitness levels were enough to get me to the top on a good day and get me down again, but I was exhausted now and we still had a mighty long trek down and off the mountain. Plus my kit, despite its quality, wasn't working. My mitts weren't good enough and my goggles were rubbish. If I went up again and the weather turned again, I was done for. And it would not only affect me but other members of the team.

Suddenly Rohan's selfless decision on Elbrus was now mine to make. I was done.

But even though I was done, I had to wait for the whole team to get off the mountain. I had five more days at 17,500 ft, a very long five days, where I would get my life back together and sort my head out.

Accepting my failure for what it was and being at peace

So when do you actually give up? Sometimes you have to face failure or a key learning along the way. Sometimes it is time to re-group; sometimes it is time to go home. I knew on Denali, and I know now, that I gave everything I had on that mountain. I was fit enough to give it one shot, and if we had had clear weather, I would have summited. I know that, and that gives me strength. However, my fitness level let me down and that will never happen again. My kit also let me down, and since then I have filled the few gaps in my arsenal. The next mountain would prove perfect for kit (well, almost) and for fitness.

So don't think of failures as failures. You also don't need to use any wishy-washy nonsense to mask it either. You take it for what it is. I tried something incredible and I put myself in a position very few people do. I did not get to the summit, but I got to Denali Pass, and if it wasn't for God's will and adverse weather, I would have summited. I am at peace with that.

Will I go back? Yes. Next time I will be fit, I will have the kit and spare goggles, and I will give plenty of time at 17,500 ft to summit. Will I get to the summit next time? Maybe, it depends on the weather and numerous other factors outside of my control. And this is the wonder and lure of mountains; you just don't know.

Such is life. Sometimes you can do everything right and prepare perfectly, but it is just not meant to be. The timing is off, the weather not right. I know experienced mountaineers who have attempted basic peaks numerous times and failed, but a novice gets up first time. This is true for business, relationships, careers, fitness and many of life's goals.

The trick is to take the lessons on the chin, adjust accordingly and go again. Maybe you don't want to do the same thing again. I will do other summits of the Big Seven before I do Denali again. But I definitely have unfinished business with this mountain.

I made the right decision. The rest of the team had another attempt two days later, and they came back battered again, this time with some serious frostbite. At that point, most of the team were done. On the last day possible, the lead guide had one more crack and my tent mate, Walt, and one of the younger guys actually made it. When he got back to the tent, he was barely recognisable. He had frostbite and could not speak or barely move. I helped him get his gear off and got him into his sleeping bag, a shadow of his former self. Having seen him in the state he was in, I knew I did not have it in me to summit on this trip in those conditions. My decision was right. I was at peace.

The decision was proven even more as the trek out was arduous. When you are nearly at the airfield glacier, you have one more hill. They call it Heartbreak Hill as it is the final straw on a very difficult trek. But the coming down was magical for me. I had totally accepted the failure and was strangely at peace with myself. The valley was incredible and we walked out on what was like a constant dawn as the sun hovered on the horizon, not quite setting, not quite rising.

Magic. And that experience empowered me for my future experiences. I now faced the new world with renewed hope, knowing I could face anything. Time to rebuild.

I now prepare for failure, a concept that was alien to me before. But it is one which needs to be explained more thoroughly so it is not misunderstood and taken as an excuse not to keep going or to try something else.

When I set goals now, I do not attach to them. I still visualise them, use my vision board, dream of them and plan for them. But I do not fixate and make them the be-all-and-end-all. I no longer use goals as an 'if I do X then I will be happy, fulfilled, complete and at peace'. (Fill your own word in there) I choose to be happy now. I have climbed Denali a thousand times in my mind and it feels wonderful. And the next time I go, I am sure that feeling will be a reality, whether I summit or not. If I don't summit, providing I gave it 100%, I won't beat myself up. I will have a wonderful experience and enjoy the journey each and every day. A summit lasts for a few minutes; life is eternal. I choose life. I choose to live in the now.

So set your goals. Go for them fully. But if life throws you a curve ball and knocks you down, *then* just get up, dust yourself off and go again. Never give up. You can maybe change direction, but take the lesson into every area of your life. The more you live and the more you push life to the very edge, the more life will push back and the more supposed failures you will face. That's life. But you need to get over them.

I have had more failure than I would like to remember in life: in relationships, business, career, money and so on. Yet I am ultimately successful in all of these areas now, and I still face little failures regularly. If you are not failing regularly, you are not stretching yourself and trying hard enough. My boss at Mars Inc., Stacey Wallace, was right when she told me that.

So go for it and stretch yourself, and be prepared to fail.

Whatever your goal, ask yourself what is the worst that can happen. Will this steer me or will this sink me? If your failure will destroy you, which is particularly applicable to business and money, then rethink. Have backups, put in caveats. Be prepared to fail, and accept it gracefully if it happens. If you walk into a situation knowing the worst possible outcome and accepting it, then go full out for the best outcome. You will become unstoppable.

So for me, it's now on to the next highest mountain. This time it is Aconcagua, Argentina, nearly 7,000 m, the highest mountain outside the Himalaya. Time for some new lessons.

Let's learn how to embrace your failures.

TRUE Thinking on

DEALING WITH FAILURE

 Shine a light on your Inner Truth

- Are you attached to your goal—do you NEED it? The only things we truly need are love, warmth, food, water and shelter; all the rest are just bonuses. Don't get so attached that your life is on hold until a certain goal is achieved: "I will be happy when…"

- Live your life today, enjoy it today and strive towards ever increasing expansion. Don't attach to your goals; use them as lights to guide you.

- When you think of your vision/goal, what do you feel?

- When you think about failure, what do you feel?

Map out your True Path

- So you have your vision and your goal, and you have your plan to get you there. What happens if you fail? Really think this through. What is the worst case scenario? And if this scenario eventuates, will it sink you?

- If it will sink you, work through backup plans and scenarios along the way to mitigate this or eliminate this. If you plan for failing, then live life every day to succeed. Then there will be fewer nasty surprises along the way.

- Map out your Plan B's and Plan C's clearly. There are many ways to get to the same result. Focus on the result, not the means of getting there, as sometimes the universe can throw you some nice surprises.

Let your True Guide lead the way

- You would not be where you are today if it wasn't for your many failures along the way. They have shaped you, and you need to believe they were for the good. What do you think your biggest failure in life has been? What did you learn from it? There has probably been many. Look now to what has served you as a result of these failures.

- What is your true belief on failure now? It may take some time to really believe that failure is inherently good, but do take small steps towards this belief, starting today. It will serve you.

- What would you rather live with: failure or regret? Think about that. One of my key mottos is: *I would much rather live with failure than regret.*

 Identify your inner True North

- If you lost all your <money> (replace this with whatever is relevant to your goal or biggest fear i.e. business, health, love), what would you have left to be grateful for? Take some time to reflect on whether these things are consistent throughout your life and how much time you spend appreciating them.

- Build gratitude into your daily life.

Chapter 10

Aconcagua

IT'S THE ADVENTURE ITSELF, NOT THE SUMMIT

*It is not because things are difficult
that we do not dare, it is because we
do not dare that they are difficult.*
~ Seneca

"I looked out onto the lake. The early morning mist was settled and peaceful, and despite the many people milling around the race start, it had an eerie calm to it. I was nervous, really nervous. I had not swum in such a deep lake before and the thought of it freaked me out a bit. Neither had I swum in such a big pack. I faced the start of my first Ironman race with trepidation. Then, as they called the competitors to the water for the long-awaited start, I looked down and realised I had made a terrible mistake."

It took me a fair while to bounce back from Denali. It shook me up enough to reconsider why I was doing mountaineering at all; a question I still struggle to answer with anything but a 'because it is there' response. With some further reflection, I can say in truth that it is because I am drawn to it in a way that is unexplainable in any logic. It is my passion, and if I did not do it, I would regret it on my deathbed. Ultimately, it is entwined into my destiny and how I am meant to serve on this planet. But I don't think I fully understand the full implication of that yet.

The draw of adventure or life goals of any kind brings with it a love/hate relationship. You are drawn to something because you love it, are passionate about it and cannot live without it. But to attain that want, lust or dream, there is a journey, a journey of adventure and exploration where you really discover who you are and what you are made of. And this journey is rarely easy. There is usually huge sacrifice, discipline and dedication along the way for any worthwhile goal.

And with that comes the inevitable doubt, whether it is creating a business, making a relationship work, competing in the Olympics or climbing a mountain. People I talk to are always interested in the final trip, the epic, the mountain itself. The adventure in reality is far, far more than that. It is an adventure of the mind from the moment you make the decision to do something and really commit to who you become.

A recent article I read, about a survey of 1,000 people on whether success was a journey or a destination, quoted 978 people as saying it was a destination. I have to admit, if you had asked me this same question ten years ago, I would have agreed. But now this statistic saddens me. My quest has taught me one key thing: it is indeed in the journey, day by day, hour by hour, where the magic truly lies. It is enjoying the now, this moment, each training run, every small mountain I climb in preparation, the decision on each piece of kit—the slow realisation of the final adventure, piece by piece. The excitement can live with you constantly if only you will let it, as the final climb and summit itself are fleeting.

In fact there is no better metaphor to use in life than mountaineering to show the importance of enjoying the journey. You spend weeks climbing to the summit, and it is indeed the first weeks and days that are the most beautiful and rewarding with the wide landscape and panoramas. If you fail to notice this along the way, you have missed out on 99% of the journey. Once it comes to Summit Day, this is the toughest and most arduous day of them all. If you are lucky, for one fleeting moment, with oxygen depleted, being knackered and only half way there (because you have to come down again), you can savour a moment of victory. A quick snapshot, five minutes to take in the scenery, a snack and it's all over. If success is indeed a destination, what a quick, sad fleeting moment in life this would be.

Rebuilding from Denali

Following Denali, I returned to financial ruin but with a smile on my face and a spring in my step as I faced the world with new eyes. I did what I had to do with the businesses and finances and rebounded, landing a great corporate job running Northern Europe and Russia for another multi-billion dollar global company. Nothing keeps me down for long. I had my positive mind switched back on and a real knowing of true wealth. Every day I wake to the cuddles of my daughter (now two), and I feel in my very soul what true wealth is. I now have the true love of my wife back too, which doubles the magic. Love magnifies the human experience. Anything I do in work or play is magnified multiple times by the love I experience in my life.

I still spent time licking my wounds physically, emotionally and mentally, but I had a whole new paradigm on life. I had faced my worst fears head-on and survived. I knew what true wealth was, and it wasn't money. I felt blessed and grateful every day.

The next couple of years would be somewhat adventure-free as I focused on rebuilding all the areas of my life from the ground up, and I could not afford any adventures, either. This time I was ensuring that the foundations being put down were solid. I had realised the first time around that I had definitely built castles on foundations of sand. I started to make my progression in my aspirations to Ironman in this time, but that is a whole new story.

Two years on, I had a need for a new adventure. The next big mountain was to be Aconcagua in the Andes, bigger than I had ever attempted before and number five of the Seven Summits. It had been booked for months, but just before I was due to go, at the very back end of the deep recession, my role in the global financial structure was in question, and I took a leap of faith in voluntary redundancy. So, going on this last adventure in this book proved to be the start of a whole new adventure in life itself. And as such it taught me the most valuable lesson of all.

Happy Christmas and goodbye

I left for South America on Christmas day! Yes, I know, not the best choice. Aconcagua has a very limited window of opportunity for climbing, and within this time frame I had limited holidays, so this was my best option. Thankfully, my very understanding wife and family let it go on this one occasion, and I made up for it in nice presents. Although the adventure has an indescribable draw, I think the hardest part as I mature is leaving my loved ones behind for three to four weeks at a time. This was never easy, but with a 2-year-old daughter added to the mix (and another on the way), it becomes a lot more difficult.

There is always the doubt factor because each time I leave I am taking a risk, a big risk. Admittedly I minimise this in every possible way, but risk it is nevertheless. But do you go through life not doing the things you dream of because there is a little risk? Some of the greatest accomplishments in all areas of life involve a little risk; it is all a matter of perception. We take a risk each time we step into our car or onto an aeroplane, but does that stop us travelling?

This time I was ready and had made my best plans to date to mitigate risk: I had chosen the best guiding company (in my opinion); I had a great kit; I was fit; and I was mentally ready. All was good. My whole vision and goal for Aconcagua was *to climb the mountain and experience a feeling of total euphoria and bliss, one I would never forget.* I aimed to totally enjoy the journey along the way and connect fully with the mountain. The actual experience will prove to astound me!

Big boots

I remember sitting in Heathrow's Terminal 4 business lounge on Christmas evening, my bare feet up on a chair, writing my journal. I had a mince pie to my right and a hot steaming cup of Christmas latte to my left. I was at peace and very much looking forward to the journey ahead. The final call came for my flight, so I had to get my huge mountaineering boots back on to get to the plane. It always causes quite a stir at airports with me lumbering through with the biggest mountaineering boots in the world, particularly at the X-ray machines where you have to take your shoes off. It takes me about ten minutes and they barely fit through the machine. It is always a necessary hassle though, as they are so big they would fill a suitcase and so heavy they would be excess baggage. Anyway, I could not bear to lose them as I would never get them replaced. So they're better off with me.

Anyway, I leant forward to pull up the zipper, as they zip from toe to knee, and as I pulled the whole zip just broke apart. I sat there stunned. These boots were bulletproof. They had brought me through Elbrus and Denali, and now they had broken whilst I was eating a mince pie! To further explain the gravity of the situation, the outer boot's zip from the toe to knee is there to protect me from the cold mostly, and on Aconcagua from the dust and rocks. This was not a good start to the trip and my peaceful resolve was shattered.

I spent hours on the flight trying to fix it with no luck. I even had an air hostess who had seamstress skills have a go. But still no luck. This was not a good start and a bad omen. This would prove even more problematic on the mountain itself. But since there was nothing I could do about it for now, I just needed to shut up because I could not put up.

Losing my salami

I flew into Chile then crossed the mountains back into Mendoza, Argentina, crossing the Andes and getting my first glimpse of Aconcagua from the plane.

It looked incredible and, more worryingly, was at the same height as the plane, which started to put the height into perspective. Aconcagua, or The Stone Sentinel as it is known, stands at a mighty 22,834 ft, the highest point outside the Himalayas. It is a notoriously difficult mountain, with the wind and sun so strong that all snow or ice is literally blown off the mountain. This makes for a very dry, notoriously windy and rather barren looking landscape, a huge contrast to previous mountain ranges.

There is some dispute over its name and origin, but one theory derives from Quechua, the local native language. They say 'akun' means 'summit', 'ka' means 'other' or 'that' and 'agua' means 'feared'. Translation: 'the high summit that is feared'. And myself and my colleagues for the trip were about to find out why.

After arriving in Mendoza, my euphoria at finding all my bags had arrived was followed by the dysphoria of having my salami confiscated at customs. I did feel a bit weird having a verbal scrap with an armed customs team over salami, but it was very special salami from my local deli and my big treat for up high. But you win some, you lose some, and I can only imagine that there was a salami feast that night in the Customs Office.

Outside the terminal I was greeted by a driver and some of the other guys on the trip. There was quite an international mix this time in the team: Dane (US) and Janos (Sweden), who would both be my tent buddies; two older guys in their 60's, Larry and John from the US, who were legends and joined my 'True Heroes list'; two South Africans, Lawrence and Shaun; two girls, Cindy (US) and Anita (Poland); Martin, another Microsoft guy from the US; a scene builder from California, Ed; and finally Andrew from Germany who would join us later.

We booked into the 5-star Hyatt in central Mendoza, did our last kit check and then took a stroll around the city, with me trying to get my boots fixed with no success. Mendoza is a lovely city, calm and serene in its parks and plazas and yet vibrant and upbeat. It is a country of meat and wine, and that seemed to be the staple diet. Considering I eat very little meat and hate red wine, it would prove a limiting factor in my food choices. And true to form, that evening we all ate together and the staple choice was steak and red wine. I had fish, much to the disapproval of the locals. It was eel, to be precise, which I must say I would never have again.

The next day we got our permits for the mountain and then drove the 100 plus miles into the heart of the Andes to Penitentes. In doing so we rose to a lofty 8,500 ft and could already feel the altitude symptoms starting to edge in. On arrival, a few of us went for a nice steady trek up one of the local hills to gain a little more altitude experience before bedtime (climb high, sleep low) and to take in the breathtaking panoramas.

That night there was more meat and wine for most and a nice early night as the next day was when the adventure was to really begin.

The adventure begins

There are several routes on Aconcagua, one of which is its own version of the Coca-Cola Trail. Following the success on Kili with the route less travelled, I opted for the Ameghino Valley's Upper Guanacos Traverse, named after the guanacos, a cousin to the lama that are frequently seen on this route. It was very much the untouched route, although a little longer and a little harder. It was harder in the sense that it was a traverse and not a typical ascent and retreat. In the latter, you can cache your gear in varying places as you go up and retrieve on the way back. For a traverse, everything needs to come up and over the mountain with you.

The next day we embarked upon the 35 mile trek into Base Camp, which would take us three days. The loads weren't too bad as we had a mule train carrying our large duffels each day, meaning we were left with day packs. Each evening we would get to camp to find the mules grazing and our bags in a big pile, and the gauchos who looked after the mules would be already drinking and roasting meat. (You will find a continual theme in the wine and meat.)

Now donkeys don't normally pose a huge threat, and I would not put them up there on my Top 10 list of scary animals. But on that trail they were lethal. Imagine the scene. You are trekking along a rocky, steep, tiny mountain pass with nowhere to really pass and very little room to manoeuvre. Then in the silence of the surrounding landscape, you start to hear a rumble, well feel it really. And then just as your senses are alerting you to something not quite right, you hear the high- pitched whistle of the gauchos and you know a barren of mules (a group of mules, which is quite appropriate given the barren landscape) is hurtling your way.

Now when I say hurtling, I really do mean hurtling, with no concept of human life. The first time I really encountered them, I was on a steep ledge and all I could do was throw myself back against the rocky pass as they careered past, one hitting me in the side of my head with one of the bags on its side. I swear it meant to do it, and I swear it chuckled as it went past. And from there on in, I had a firm eye out for the killer donkeys and their mischievous ways.

That evening we camped at Pampa de Lenas Camp at 8,910 ft. The stars were out, the air was warm and the feeling was almost like a park BBQ as the local gauchos were cooking large steaks on an open fire. When in Rome … so that night I joined in on the meat extravaganza but passed on the flowing red wine. Yet again, here the mountain guides showed a propensity to be able to drink and smoke, get up and still kick your arse the next day — amazing. I was also introduced to 'yerba mate', a local tea which is served in a gourd and drunk with a metal straw called a 'bombilla'. I thought it tasted like piss but smiled gratefully anyway. We also got to mingle with the local gauchos, the cowboys of the South American pampas who were hard as nails. They really put our poncy trip in perspective. Still, they thought we were mental at looking to climb The Feared One. That gave perspective.

The Feared One!

As I was thinking about The Feared One, a guy emerged from the tent behind us. He stretched widely as if emerging from a deep, deep sleep and then noticed me. "G'day mate," he drawled in a deep Aussie twang. We chatted for a while and what I discovered was somewhat daunting and debilitating. He was quite an accomplished climber and guide who had been on the mountain for three weeks. He had been buffeted with storms, battered by the winds and beaten by the unbelievable arid atmosphere. He had not slept in weeks and had finally given up on a summit attempt as the weather was too bad. Just the motivational pep talk I needed. As I sat there listening to his tale, I could not help but notice how worn out he looked, how dried out, how exhausted, like he had just been to war. As the next few weeks would unfold, I would realise that he pretty much had.

The next day was much like the first, with added river crossings and not seeing anyone else all day. We had the whole mountain range to ourselves, and I was alone with myself and my thoughts. It was a beautiful day, and despite the barren, high desert landscape, it had a certain beauty to it and an element of serenity. The Andes were rising ever more magnificently to our left, and by the end of the day we finally got a glimpse of Aconcagua itself. It was massive, bigger than anything I had ever seen, and was both exciting and hugely scary at the same time. We arrived at camp, Casa de Piedra (The Stone House), and everyone ate and bedded down quite quickly as it had been a long two-day trek, and tomorrow the climbing began properly. I was feeling good; I was feeling confident; I was feeling serene. But that was all about to change.

In the night I started to develop a fever. I recognised it from my experience on the banks of the Snowy River, and I had a rough night. The fever quickly went to my chest and I was starting to cough up phlegm.

Thankfully, I had brought drugs for a chest infection and to help with fever (preparation at its greatest), and I started taking them in the middle of the night. As such, by morning I felt remarkably okay considering and cracked on without a second thought.

The climbing begins and the trip is nearly all over

The highlight of the next day was the start, as we had to cross the rapids of the icy cold glacial river. We had two options, and some of the guys chose Option One, which was to strip off and wade through. I chose Option Two, the easy route of bribing the gauchos to take me over on the back of a mule. Getting on a mule and then trusting it enough to let it take you across a raging river is quite a feat. Part way across, I swear it winked at me and I recognised it! It was the psycho donkey that nearly killed me on the path the previous day. Anyway, I arrived safe and dry to live another day.

That day we continued to rise to Base Camp — a gruelling 1,000 m gain in total. I was remarkably strong and stayed in the front group for most of the way. Part way up, I glanced skyward to catch my first glimpse of condors, magnificent, truly majestic birds, soaring through the air. All was good, or so it seemed.

As the day progressed, I deteriorated, at first slowly and then rapidly. I was running hot when I shouldn't be and cold when I shouldn't be. The fever was returning and getting worse. We were of course gaining altitude and my chest was being punished simultaneously. I was coughing more and more until it was a hacking cough and I was bringing up phlegm. Then about forty minutes before Base Camp, I suddenly felt as weak as a kitten and collapsed on the ground.

Everyone else went on. I was left in tatters with just one of the guides. I continued at a crawl. My chest was rattling as I coughed up sputum and spat it into the wind. It was nearly 4,000 m and I obviously had a chest infection. Next to a broken leg, this is the worst infliction you can have up here.

Slowly but surely I got to Base Camp that day with the help of the guide who had stayed to help me in.

I was not in good shape. The one saving grace about this base camp was there was a doctor there to whom I went straight to see. The diagnosis was not good: deep bronchial chest infection, high fever (40 degrees) and high blood pressure, all of which are disastrous at this altitude. Was this attempt over before it had even begun? Unless I had a miracle, I was going back down with the killer donkeys.

I went back to my tent for a long think, and it was a long think indeed. I spent the whole night in a fever with a relentless hacking cough. The dry, arid air and altitude wasn't helping it either. I was very neutral about things though, in a strange, removed way. It was no longer about the summit and the failure. It was about getting well. I had already faced fever on the Snowy River, failure on Denali and severe diarrhea in the desert. I had gotten through all of those, and I would get through this. It is amazing how your resilience builds with experience, and you gain a sense of knowing beyond believing.

The power of intention

It was time for the power of the mind. The power of positive thought. The power of intention. I was fit. I had brought the right drugs, so my preparation was perfect. This was happening in the perfect place as we were in Base Camp with a doctor, and we had three days of rest and cache before any decisions needed to be made. I rested, took the drugs diligently, hydrated well and sat in the mess tent for most of the next day, inhaling steam from a bowl to try and clear my lungs. You could tell by the comments from everyone around me that I was already written off—some even wishing me well and saying preliminary goodbyes. There is a lesson there: Never write off a Welshman! Surprisingly, it wasn't me who dropped first. Whilst I was in my own world of potential recovery, Larry was having his own problems.

On the second day I was feeling better, but not well enough to join the team on an exploratory jaunt up to the next level of altitude and back. I just watched them go. Time to kick back and enjoy Base Camp - Internet, phone, shower.

Yes, a shower! I could not believe it. So off I went with my twenty dollars and a towel to see what this was really about. In a big, square, battered, tent with plastic sheeting on the floor, like some macabre torture room, was the luxurious shower suite. Now the shower itself was quite a contraption. Imagine a big bag with a hole in it hanging from the ceiling and a plastic pipe coming out with a hose you put your thumb over to squirt water over you. Voila. Western world insult, but here with warmish water, total luxury! That's the best twenty dollars I have spent at 4,200 m, and it left me refreshed and re-invigorated.

Toilets up here were similar to the wooden huts on Kilimanjaro, only these were metal and the stench wasn't quite so bad due to the cold, arid air. However, one thing to note is to be very careful when you have sunglasses propped up on your head. One of the team made the school boy error of knocking them off their head by mistake, right down the toilet hole. These glasses were much needed for Summit Day; hence, he had to go fishing. Not nice.

On the third day the team went up to the next camp to cache their gear. I still wasn't ready, but I had a feeling that I might be the next day. And the next day was D-Day as I needed to see the doctor in order to be signed off or I was off the mountain. More rest, more steam inhalation, more mind control.

Once in a blue moon

That night was like some mystical sign from the heavens because not only was it New Year's Eve but there was also a blue moon. This won't happen again for another twenty years.

So my chances of recovery were slim, so slim it was a 'once in a blue moon' chance. And here one was — the irony. I smiled up at the heavens and the glorious full moon: a blue moon, a new year, a new life, new chances and opportunities. What better sign.

The following morning I got signed off by the doctor as a miraculous recovery but with some scepticism, as if I had done something weird. I was given the go ahead to go on. So up I went. Thankfully, I was able to hire a porter to help with bags as I had missed a cache, but all in all things were good. We sent the mule train back down the mountain, and now we were on our own on the high slopes of Aconcagua. The big magic boots had come this far by mule, and now on the high slopes we made attempts to fix them, with no real luck. Hence, I spent the rest of the mountain with my right boot gaffer taped.

Whilst I was still focused on recovery, the rest of the team was falling apart. Team bitching and moaning had started at Base Camp, and there were many strong characters with many different opinions on how to tackle the mountain. The poor guides were getting grilled and constantly second-guessed. The whole atmosphere was becoming unbearable. I wasn't getting involved and chose to enjoy my journey, which I thoroughly was. To top it off, by the final day Larry had to go back down the mountain with a combination of back problems and altitude symptoms. He was done, which was a sad loss as he was one of the nicest and most positive in the group.

Some individuals wanted a detailed itinerary of exactly when things would happen. Other people wanted different meals, like it was some holiday camp. This was worrying as this wasn't a field trip and the mountain holds no schedule. People want it all now, wanting convenience, wanting the mountain delivered up in a package with money back guarantees. Mountaineering doesn't work like that, neither does life.

Back in the game

So I was ready to face the mountain. All eyes were on me to see how long I would last. The next climb up to Camp 1 was a steep one and full of penintentes. These are giant icicles formed by wind and sun that tower higher than a man. It was strangely eerie, trekking through these giant ice fields in which small paths had been carved that barely fitted a man and a pack. It felt like a graveyard of ice tombstones in the largely barren and dry surrounding landscape. I enjoyed that day, savouring each moment because I was just climbing again and nothing else mattered. Each day now was a bonus, and I would see as much of the mountain as I could. I was focused on the magnificent feeling of climbing the mountain and the elation and euphoria that comes with it, in the now. What a metaphor and beautiful lesson for life itself.

Camp 1 was at 15,200 ft and you could now really start to feel the altitude. We were also out of the shelter of the mountain and very exposed on the high slopes, so the wind was about to introduce itself fully. The toilet system had now changed too, as from here on in we needed to do Number Twos in a bag. Yes, a bag. Biodegrading can literally take centuries in the cold, arid climate, so all poo has to come off the mountain. More on that later.

It was so dry and arid now that you would wake every hour with your tongue stuck to the roof of mouth. It was soon cracked right down the middle. I had bigger things to worry about, though, as my tent mates were now suffering and falling apart themselves. But first we had to get the tent secured with rock walls. This was the strange contrast of Aconcagua. Instead of having ice walls to protect you, you needed to build rock ones out of the barren landscape. And you needed huge rocks to secure the tent with as you could not get a peg in the ground if you tried.

We started off with smaller rocks and the guide soon came over and encouraged much bigger ones.

Thankfully, we took the advice, otherwise the tent might not have been there in the morning and neither would we.

That night the wind picked up, and it blew so hard it felt like an elephant sitting against the side of the tent.

At times it became so maniacal you really thought the whole thing could be picked up and blown off the mountain with you in it. It was terrifying. Next day, despite the howling winds and much resistance from the team, we went up to do our next cache. At times that day, I was leaning full tilt into the wind with my full weight, driving forward in my old rugby manner in fear that one more gust and I would be done. Dane did not join us that day as he was now suffering with altitude sickness badly, and diarrhoea too, meaning we were now all at risk also.

The next day as we prepared to go to Camp 2, Dane decided he had had enough. This was incredibly sad news as he was a great member of the team and the one I bonded with the most. He was also the most upbeat next to Larry. So it felt like we were losing all the positive energy in a rapidly infighting team, and it was about to get worse.

Literally pissing in the wind

The winds had died down the following day, allowing us to move to Camp 2 in relatively normal conditions. Camp 2 lay at a lofty 17,800 ft (5,400 m), and now altitude sickness was starting to kick in proper throughout the group. Ever since my near departure, I had been somewhat serene and just enjoying each day as it came, classing it as an added bonus. I was just waiting for my chest infection to finally peter out. But even here I was feeling remarkably okay. I was breathless and had difficulty in sleeping for more than thirty minutes at a time, but that wasn't unusual. I had been warned by the doctor that my chest would not and could not heal in this high altitude, so I was playing a dangerous game.

There was no water to be found this high up except for a frozen river of ice that cascaded across the rocks next to the camp. In order to fill bottles, you would tentatively make your way across the ice and then listen in the silence of the mountain for a gurgle, any sign of water trickling below. Then once you had located it, you took your ice axe to the ice and hacked down relentlessly to where the source was.

If you were lucky, you found some. As the holes were relatively small, you then had to scoop up small amounts to bring up to your main water bottle. The whole procedure could take ages, and combined with accumulating lethargy from the altitude and winds, it was no small feat. I am now very grateful every time I just turn on a tap.

The winds picked up again that afternoon, and we were buffeted with the terrifying force again. In the midst of it all, I needed the toilet. Shit. Once again, when a man's gotta go, a man's gotta go.

Like all other adventures, to get out of the tent you need to get fully robed in all weather gear, especially when you have 100 mph winds careering down the mountain.

I then fought my way across to the only set of large rocks remotely sheltered from the destructive gales. As I huddled down behind them, the wind was still coming in from all sides, strangely able to manipulate the mountain so that no nook or cranny was safe. Now I needed the toilet bad. Firstly, Number One, and now I truly know the power of the phrase 'pissing in the wind'. I had to be extra vigilant as the wind was constantly changing. (I think most of me was covered in pee to some extent by the end of the trip.)

The biggest challenge, however, was Number Two. Now bearing in mind you have to get in position whilst wearing full mountain gear, this is no small feat. The wind is lapping all around and now you need to poo in a bag, very carefully too, as getting your aim wrong could mean the 'shit would hit the fan' (or indeed the wind). Now just getting all the above right is one thing, but then you need to navigate the toilet paper and wiping aspect; trying to control a piece of tissue in a raging storm is some challenge. On this attempt, I was indeed successful and mightily impressed with my skills. Further up the mountain, I would not be so lucky when I lose my toilet bag and only have a Ziploc.

Back to the tent exhausted. Just going to the toilet at this altitude totally takes it out of you, but a celebration was in order. So I cracked out some treats in the form of chilli crackers and Green and Black's Organic Milk Chocolate. Happy Toilet Day!

Another one bites the dust

The next day we went to cache up to High Camp, Piedras Blancas (White Rocks) at 19,200 ft. To put this cache, and indeed the next camp, into perspective, we were now at the height of Kilimanjaro and higher than Elbrus and Denali. This is where we were going to camp the next few days. I felt okay, far better than on any of the other mountains and also a lot better than other members of the group, who were now all suffering to some extent from headaches and other more serious altitude symptoms. We took a brief rest, cached some gear and then came straight back down.

As we were lying in the tent, I started to notice Janus was behaving strangely. The guide came in to check on us and Janus said everything was okay, but I knew it wasn't. I quizzed him further, and he could not string a coherent sentence together. His coordination was all over the place. I remembered what I was like on Kili and also knew how dangerous it was. Yet he could not see it himself, just as I could not on Kili; that is the danger of high altitude. I called for the lead guide and he came to do a full assessment; the signs were not good. The key indicator was oxygen saturation and Janus' was at 55%. Most people at normal levels are 99%, and if you are hitting mid-seventies on mountains, it is a danger sign. My ex-wife is an Accident and Emergency Doctor and stats in the seventies is a danger sign to her. So this was very serious. Within hours he was off the mountain, and I was alone in the tent. Quarter of the team had now dropped.

How things had turned around in a few days. I had been the one nearly done and with all bets against me; now I was the only one left in my tent. Things on the mountain can change in a heartbeat, as can life. Martin moved into the tent that afternoon, thank goodness, as with just me I think it would have blown away that night.

Summit Day

The next day we moved up to High Camp and prepared for summit. Three were already gone and half of the remaining team were not in good shape. Plus the weather was deteriorating. We had the next day as rest day, although you can hardly rest when camping at the height of Kili. My heart rate was high, in the mid-nineties, and sleep was now non-existent. Sleep deprivation is a huge issue at this altitude.

The biggest battle at this height was getting water, and the guides were constantly boiling snow and ice. It was so, so dry up here. It was like being in the Sahara whilst sitting on top of Kili—a combination I would not wish on anyone.

My mouth was so dry and with my nose still blocked with infection I could only breathe through my mouth and would wake every twenty minutes. My lips, tongue and mouth were so dry, cracked and swollen that I had to dribble a little water from my bottle just to unstick them before I could move them. It was surreal.

Despite the hardship, I still felt pretty good considering I shouldn't have been there. I should have gone down a long time ago, and yet there I was now looking like one of the strongest in the group. That evening we were going for summit, so it was time to prepare. I decided I would just do my best and enjoy the journey.

Like most Summit Days, it started at midnight in the biting cold of high altitude. As we started off, everything felt good. My kit was perfect. I was feeling good then … pop, pop. I had new bib-fronted down trousers for the trip for extra warmth, only to be used on Summit Day (they look like very big dungarees).

They seemed to fit perfectly at home, but I had not tested them in 'real conditions'. So the poppers on the sides and back just kept un-popping at the slightest movement: taking off pack, putting on pack, bending down. In the end I had to just leave it as is, with my trousers wide open on the side and my arse exposed. Given all my preparation, I was more than frustrated. Despite my diligent preparation, one little thing like a little popper can screw up an attempt like Aconcagua. I was determined not to let it get to me, and so I cracked on regardless, arse flapping in the wind. Such is life.

You can only prepare so much. There will always be little elements to throw you curve balls along the way. The quality of your life is dependent on how you react to those curve balls. I choose to throw mine back and get on with it.

The stars were out and, as is usual at such heights, the sky was magnificent. It was bitterly cold though, and with wind chill it must have been -30. But to me it was all relative. I had good kit now (bar the trousers and boots) and I had experienced the Denali Pass, so this did not faze me.

Within hours, Ed, Lawrence, John and Shaun had all dropped out. The altitude was too much. There was only five left: Cindy, Anita, Martin, Andrew and me. I was now the highest I had ever been by a long way, way higher even than the dizzy heights of Kilimanjaro, each step a new adventure into the unknown.

The high altitude was taking its toll as each step seemed to get slower and slower and each breath deeper and deeper to get the same miniscule amount of oxygen relief. But as I plodded towards the summit, I felt a strange sense of peace. This wasn't the gruelling attempts I had experienced before. It was tough yes, very tough, but I was in a different place with this mountain. I wasn't there to conquer it, to do battle and summit no matter what. I was there to experience the magic of it, to get as high as it would let me. My whole vision for Aconcagua was to climb the mountain and experience a feeling of total euphoria and bliss, one I would never forget. I was in her domain now.

As we approached the ridge of the next key milestone, Independencia at 20,790 ft, I glanced upwards for the first time in thirty minutes, as I had only been focused on my feet. As I looked towards what must be Independencia, I stopped instantly and gasped, not for air but in awe at what I saw. Was it a vision? Was it real? Or was I going mad? ... Even with the effects of the altitude, it shocked me so much I stumbled and fell to one knee.

There I was, on the heights of Aconcagua, the highest point I had ever reached, on one knee in front of ... a burning bush.

The burning bush

I felt a surge of euphoria and bliss wash over me as I gazed into the flames of the burning bush in front of me. Nobody was behind me for some way, and people in front were all too busy focusing on their own next step, oblivious to what I was witnessing. I knelt there and took in the experience. My logical mind took over and started to ring alarm bells; this was altitude, after all. This must be an illusion; snap out of it. I stood up and gazed more intently. I shook my head and closed my eyes to shrug it off. But on opening my eyes it was still there, a bush burning so bright, so magnificent, so pure, so amazing.

I don't know how long I stood there, totally captured in the magic of it all. But it must have been some time as I was nudged by someone behind to move on. I turned and said, "Do you see that?"

They looked directly at me and then directly at the bush and said, "Yes, that's Independencia," and moved past me.

I don't know what the sign was. It was sunrise and could have been an illusion. It could have been from the altitude, or indeed pure madness. But nothing can describe the feeling I had there. It was what I had come for.

On returning to Britain, the true meaning of Independencia struck home more fully. It is the Spanish word for 'independence', the true meaning of which is 'freedom from control, influence and support of others'. And in that moment I had experienced true freedom from my summit goals and was returning home to running my own companies again. The serendipity of experiencing that moment, at that time in my life, at that point on the mountain, is breathtaking.

Shortly after we summited to Independencia, 20,790 ft, I saw an abandoned wooden hut standing proudly exactly where I had seen the bush. It was covered in prayer flags. The energy of the place was magnificent. We all rested for a while whilst the guide took in the options to summit. The weather was closing in and was quite fierce now. We were in the eye of a storm. I don't know what everyone else was thinking, but I was completely spaced out after my spiritual experience and just enjoying the moment. Despite bad reports and people starting to trickle back from failed attempts at the summit, we decided as a group to proceed. I no longer cared, but was happy to go along for the ride.

We then climbed a near vertical glacial pass and entered El Paso del Viento (Pass of the Wind), which was eerie and dark, bathed entirely in shadow. With only five of us left, we battled our way across the pass. And I mean battle. The wind was so strong now, I was leaning my full weight into it, step by tiny step. Each step was being secured with a trekking pole and ice axe as some security against being blown off the mountain. This was the most intense experience of wind yet for me, far greater than the sandstorms of the Sahara, far more powerful than the howling gales in the Denali Pass. Yet I maintained calm and serene through it all.

Halfway along, we were starting to get people ahead of us turning back and passing us. They had had enough. When finally one of those came back with frostbite, it was time for a retreat, and retreat we did.

On reaching High Camp, three of the remaining five were done. They were immediately packing up to get off the mountain to join the four that went back earlier. That left two of us. I lay in the tent contemplating what I had just witnessed, trying to process it and make sense of it. But in the highs of altitude, I could not think straight ... but I did feel good.

Meanwhile, Cindy was devastated by the failure and was kicking up a storm herself in trying to force the hands of the guides for another summit bid. Strangely, I felt okay physically and was actually up for another go. So we kicked back and waited for weather reports. In the meantime, we found out that some people made it up that day despite the storms and raging wind. That intensified Cindy's feelings even further.

As we waited, I lay back in the tent with a sense of freedom, peace and joy. I had overcome huge obstacles on this mountain. I had enjoyed each step of the way and really immersed myself in the mountain itself. I had experienced a profound, spiritual moment that I still could not quite fathom. I had come prepared and proved everything I needed to, to myself. And here I was — one of the last two of twelve. I did not need the summit to feel complete. The weather reports came in. A huge storm was about to descend, worse than we had experienced already. Yet again, we were in God's hands. My trip was done; the risk was no longer worth it. I had had my magical summit feeling without the need of the summit. I had reached the highest point in my life to date and for that I could celebrate.

Cindy, however, was devastated. Such differing thoughts and emotions in exactly the same moment. I was happy, blissful almost, from my experience. Cindy, on the other hand, was raging, mad and bitter. One person's heaven is another person's hell. Like the hell I had created for myself on Denali.

We packed up and got off the mountain as quickly as possible. We completed the traverse, going over the other side of the mountain down to Plaza de Mulas. It was a huge drop in altitude with some massive slopes and steep, careering descents. Having had the peace and solitude of the route we took, it came as quite a shock to see Plaza de Mulas. A whole shanty town emerged on the landscape below, a scattering of tin huts and tents everywhere. A small town in its own right that looked positively industrial, it was nestled on the landscape of the surrounding beauty. On arriving, we had pizza waiting, water, juice and hot tea a plenty, plus cakes and biscuits. It was like arriving in heaven itself. I also discovered the highest art gallery in world on the way to the toilet and bought a picture. My trip was just getting better and more comical by the moment.

We camped there that night, and then the following day we loaded our remaining gear back onto new mules and trekked an exhausting death march of some eight hours out of the valley. Despite my exhaustion, I really enjoyed this last bit, taking in the beauty and saying my farewells to the mountain that had taught me so much. The surrounding landscape was stunning on this side of the mountain, such a contrast to the other side. The geology was amazing with so many different rock formations and colours, as if the world itself was created here in this deep valley in the depths of the Andes. It was like God herself had used it to test all the different rock formations to see which looked prettiest. I picked up a fantastic piece of rock that looked just like a brain, a reminder to me of the power of the mind. It weighed about 4 kg and I carried that rock six hours out. It now sits on my desk as a daily reminder.

Now, do you remember those climbers who actually made the summit? We saw those summiteers back in Mendoza days later, all with severe frost bite on hands and face. I knew then, even more, that we'd made the right decision. I like my nose even if it has been broken more times than I care to remember. But other members of the team were moaning and bitching about not summiting and threatening to put in complaints, looking to blame something or someone. How sad.

How do you sue a mountain? How do you sue the weather? Surrounded by such beauty, and yet the inner turmoil was making the experience a hell, not a heaven. Such is our choice in our life experience; I choose heaven.

It is the experience, not the summit. It is the many, many moments along the way, not a moment. It is the feeling you can feel at any point just by taking a deep breath and absorbing the wonder. Not a feeling you only get by achieving something. Success truly is a journey, not a destination. I did not deserve to summit Denali as I wasn't mentally ready for it or fully prepared. I did deserve to summit Aconcagua, but I did not need to as the feeling I got by my experiencing that magical moment far surpassed the feeling of any summit. So, although we strive for our goals, sometimes God will deliver something far greater along the way if we just remain open to it. Despite the goals themselves, we need to learn to detach from the outcomes. And that is the next great adventure.

Time for new adventures!

TRUE Thinking on

LIVING THE ADVENTURE NOW

 Shine a light on your Inner Truth

- How would you like to be remembered as a person? What impression do you want to leave? What is to be your legacy? Whose life is better for you having been here? Write the message for your tombstone. Is it one you are proud of?

- Note your feelings every day in every moment.

  Notice what makes you happy and do more of it. Note what makes you unhappy, really notice, and either change it or do less of it. Try to make it so that you can love it. I hate doing expenses, but now I make it a game, and I give myself a reward at the end of it. Anything can be fun if you give it enough attention and focus.

Map out your True path

- Look for the positive. One person's heaven is another person's hell; you choose. Consciously choose and create your own heaven.

- Think now about something you are quite negative about. Seek the positives; really seek them out. Look for the silver lining and make this a habit. Become consciously aware when you are starting to bitch or moan and stop it. Always look to the positive. How can you see the good in every day?

- Write a motto to remind yourself of how to live every day. For example: 'Everything happens in perfect time.' Or 'Every day in every way, I get better and better'

Let your True Guide lead the way

- Mirror. Write down a list of people that you have had a positive impact on and what you did to serve them. This can be the smallest thing. I like to have fun and make people smile. That in itself is a gift every single day. If you cannot think of too many people you have had a positive influence on, make it your goal, then, to go out today and make a difference. No excuses, even if it is just a smile. Believe you can make a difference every day ... because it is true.

- Find a way of appreciating and recognising the journey every day, rather than always just focusing on the end result. Believe in the day, for it is in the day that the magic happens.

Identify your inner True North

- In which ways do you feel connected to a higher source, a greater power, every day? For example, meditation, religion, music, art or exercise. Whatever is your source, connect to it daily to constantly realign yourself to **life's great adventure** and to experience and enjoy the journey in its fullest form every single day.

- What feelings do you want to feel now? How can you bring more of this feeling into your life in every moment? On the train and tube, I listen to uplifting music to keep me smiling. Music is a wonderful way to experience feelings in the now, be it relaxation with classical music or excitement with rock. You choose your feeling.

The great adventure continues...

*It is more important to know where you
are going than to get there quickly.
~ Mabel Newcomber*

And so the adventures for this book have come to an end, but the adventures in life are only just beginning as I apply these lessons to all the areas of life. There are some even bigger adventures to come.

What have we really learned during our adventures together?

We started this journey defining our passions and learning to step into what we love to do. We looked to create visions for our life goals and life roles, to define what we will be, do and have. We looked at creating goals and then stepping into them, one step at a time; to plan and prepare and have the patience to see the fruits of our labour. We have dealt with the fear you will face along the way, as well as the tough decisions that will no doubt have to be made, and then we dealt with failure itself.

Finally, we came full circle and realised it is not about the goals, although you need to set them. It is not about the vision, although you need a powerful one. It is about the essence of the journey and enjoying each precious moment along the way. It is about being aligned with the absolute knowing that you are creating and progressing towards being the best you can ultimately be.

I keep pushing the boundaries, knowing I am living full out, knowing that I can die potentially with many failures under my belt, but with no regrets. That to me is life.

I have shared the raw truth with you. I have not dressed it up in any way, and along the way I have bared my soul, sharing intimate moments and profound moments. I did this so you can see I am no hero. I am a very ordinary guy who has persevered and failed along the way to achieve some extraordinary things. I am no super athlete; I have built up fitness from very humble beginnings. I have written this not to impress you, but to impress upon you your own unlimited, latent ability that may lay dormant and to urge you to follow your passions.

I started this adventure with huge EGO, with a burning determination and resolve, and although I have achieved some incredible things, I did so the hard way. As such I missed a lot of the beauty in my earlier journeys. I no longer attach to the goals themselves. I attach to the feeling the goals are likely to give me and then remain open to when and how that feeling will come. And sometimes it comes in the most magical and unexpected ways. It is no longer about the summit, the million pounds or the toys. It is about the feelings I experience every single day. Every single moment.

Success is the journey, not the destination; I truly believe that. My experiences have really highlighted a key flaw in the classical goal setting methodology of the 21st century, that is to set big goals, drive hard, do it fast and then set bigger goals. And I am guilty as anyone in doing this in my early days. But do you truly enjoy the journey? And what happens when you get your goal? More often than not, you don't notice as you have already set bigger goals. Kilimanjaro had been a dream of mine for years and, yes, I climbed it. But did I enjoy it? The trip, yes. The experience, yes.

But the Summit Day? It was pure hell and I made it so. 'Pole pole' could have made Kili's Summit Day truly memorable, and I would be able to picture and feel the experience to this day.

It is not about what I want in life, what I desire. It is about what I deserve. For if I give enough, serve enough and love what I do enough, I will then deserve everything I can possibly imagine in life and more.

Being a book on adventure, you would think it a battle of the body, of physical endurance and of stamina.

What my adventures have taught me more than anything else is that it is a battle of the mind, daily. Our mind is the one thing that totally governs us every single second of every single day. We need to recognise this and take back control of our own minds and with it our destiny. Weed out those negative thoughts one by one. Eradicate the fearful thoughts piece by piece and step into the life you desire.

The mind is all-powerful, and it is the one thing within our control. We might not be able to dictate external events, but we can control how we think about them. The more I learn and the more I discover about the mind, the more amazed I become. I still have much to learn, and this will be central to life's next great adventure as we venture further down the rabbit hole.

So that brings me to today and my next plans. I am sure they will change somewhat, but the adventure continues. What next? Well, since I now have my second daughter, I don't really want to be away much whilst she is very young, so it will be the Ironman. This is an endurance feat that still scares the shit out of me, and that's exactly why I want to do it — to see if I can.

What is the Ironman? A 2.2 mile swim in open water, a 112 mile bike ride on a hilly course, followed by a full 26 mile marathon. All to be completed in less than 17 hours. And I have two main issues in this challenge: I cannot really swim, and I have not been on a bike since I was a kid.

Then we have Everest, the Poles and probably a return to Denali to put some demons to rest. Perhaps the Jungle Marathon thrown in too. You will have to wait and see…

Whatever the adventure, life's great lessons continue to evolve, and the next adventure is going to be even more exhilarating. Come join me.

In the meantime, yours in adventure…

Deri ap John Llewellyn-Davies

Quotation Locations

Pp 1, 27 - www.inspirational-quotes.info/inspirational-quotes-1.html

Pg 47 - www.brainyquote.com/quotes/quotes/g/eorgebern109542.html

Pg 63 - www.quotationspage.com/quote/3141.html

Pg 85 - www.quotationspage.com/quote/24004.html

Pg 113 - www.goodreads.com/quotes/show/33052

Pg 141 - www.inspirational-quotes.info/failure.html

Pg 161 - www.behappy101.com/success-quotes.html

Pg 183 - www.quotefancy.com/quote/1363804

Pg 207 - www.inspirationpeak.com/courage.html

Pg 239 - www.goodreads.com/quotes/show/304211

About the Author

Deri Llewellyn-Davies

SPEAKER, AUTHOR, ADVENTURER & ENTREPRENEUR

Deri Llewellyn-Davies is an internationally acclaimed speaker, author, adventurer and entrepreneur who is transforming lives around the world with his core focus on Business, Life and High performance and how they are intrinsically linked.

One of the truly unique aspects of his speeches comes from his love of adventure. As he shares in his first book, Life's Great Adventure, Deri has climbed six of the highest mountains in the world, run the Marathon des Sables, and completed an IronMan. He also lived to tell his tale of "No Regrets" after surviving the devastating earthquake while climbing Everest in the spring of 2015 as shared in his hugely popular TEDx presentation.

In a career spanning two decades, Deri's business expertise has included roles on elite corporate boards through four billion dollar companies up to European executive board level. Having run several of his own businesses, advising over 300 boards and speaking to thousands of business owners he brings his audiences deep insights with both a global and local perspective on business and life.

To learn more about Deri, or to book him as a speaker, head here:
www.deri.live

To create your own epic life plan, head here:
www.diamondlifedesign.com